MW01488005

THE SPIRITED FESTIVAL

(The Bachelor Preacher's Mystery Series)

By

BOB WYATT

xulon PRESS

DEDICATION

This book is dedicated to Maudie Williams who was always a source of encouragement to those around her. I frequently received her freshly baked chocolate chip cookies with a word of advice and direction when she thought I was making a wrong turn in my life. Her service to God and the Church was unmistakable as she demonstrated the Scripture from Philippians 2:13, "I can do all things thru Christ who strengthens me."

CHAPTER ONE

*H*i, *I'm Jack Temple, minister of the local Nickerson Street Church. Yes, you guessed it. I'm single. I'm a bachelor preacher, but that doesn't mean I'm not involved in a lot of people's lives. Each one of the congregation has had a special mystery in their life that has brought me closer to knowing them and participating in their life.*

Take Dollie Burgess for example. Dollie is one of the members here at Nickerson Street Church. She is a saint. There are not enough good things to say to let you know exactly how important she is to the congregation and community. She would do anything to help someone. Her willingness to share what she has and to encourage a person at the same time is as natural as breathing for her. She always seems to bring us back to the Bible when we have lost the way. She knows what God would have us do.

"Whew, glad that's done," remarked Dollie Burgess.

Dollie shook her head to throw her hair back and wiped her brow with a paper towel.

"Three cakes for Amy Rogers," she said as she went over a written list of the orders she had for her catering business.

Nodding approval at all she had done, she launched into a last minute inventory to insure that everything was complete. With one hand she counted the baked items but still managed with her other hand to give a lift to the window above the sink to let in some fresh cool evening air and to allow the oven heat to escape. She looked at the ceiling fan with a frown and made a mental note to ask Rev. Temple to repair it for her.

Outside she heard the sound of a barking dog and the roar of a car racing down Main Street in Sassafras Springs, Missouri. The sounds brought her back to the reality of the world outside her kitchen. It would soon be time for her to go to choir practice at the church and she needed to complete the inventory of the baked goods before she left.

Her dress revealed the long hours she had been cooking and baking in the kitchen, particularly her apron that had been used both as a wipe cloth and a hot pad. The apron was stained with various food colorings and flavorings. Yet as she looked at the colorfully stained apron, she chuckled with a smile. She could see a Picasso or some other master's work on canvass in that apron.

"I wonder if my apron will fetch a great price at an art auction some day?" she laughed.

Drops of perspiration rolled down her forehead and into her eyes making her blink. She checked a couple of places on the calendar and scratched out one line. "Now did I miss anything?" she questioned.

Dollie is one of those slightly passed middle age, slightly overweight, slightly out-going people who was the source of strength for a lot of people in the community. Her bright eyed smiling face beamed underneath the red haired mop that topped her head.

This bright cheerful lady served the church as treasurer and most recently had become Jack Temple's landlord. Jack was a lifesaver for her as he had repaired a number of things around the house. He mowed the yard where the grass seemed to grow faster every year. He repaired the back screen that kept falling apart. He had even tackled washing the front window that had made everything outside look nicer and caused her to change her mind about going to the optometrist about new glasses.

Wiping a paper towel across her face Dollie checked the calendar laying flat on the counter with a puzzled look. Nodding occasionally, she pointed her finger at the baked goods and then to the calendar. One by one she checked the list to verify that everything had been completed for the day.

Being satisfied, she picked up a box from the pantry, lined it with aluminum foil, and without stopping to think about how unseasonably hot outside it was she started placing a layered cake in a box to take to her neighbor Julia Ferguson.

The neighbor lady was celebrating her 90th birthday the next day and Dollie wanted to help her celebrate it by surprising her with a decorated cake. The Sunday before at church Dollie had encouraged the congregation to send birthday cards. That was the way Dollie was. She was constantly finding ways to encourage and help others.

Dollie chuckled as she wiped her hands on the red, white and blue apron that Mrs. Ferguson had given her. She remembered thinking "When will I ever wear that thing?" but it had become her favorite apron to use when preparing baked goods.

The apron was made of terrycloth and perfect to wear when working in the kitchen. The material absorbed the moisture on her hands and the apron was easily washed and dried. In fact, Dollie was looking to buy some like it. She had used the apron earlier in the month for a patriotic President's Day reception at the city hall. Mrs. Ferguson was at the event and Dollie saw Mrs. Ferguson's smile when she saw the apron. The apron was perfect for the occasion and considering the number of patriotic events in the area Mrs. Ferguson had made an excellent choice.

New drops of perspiration beaded up and started to roll down Dollie's forehead. Her face looked like she was crying but she charged on with her work. She took another paper towel in one hand and the bank's complimentary calendar in the other. Wiping her face, she checked the scribbled notes on the calendar.

The local Sassafras Springs Savings & Loan gave customers calendars at Christmas and Dollie had found the calendar to be perfect for keeping her records for the catering business. Each date had a nice size square that gave her room to write the orders as she got them. She had the calendar hanging next to the telephone with a pencil on a string to make sure there was something handy to write with when an order would be called in.

Her brother, Carl, had urged her to get a record keeping book for bookkeeping purposes, but Dollie thought that the transition from calendar to book was just unnecessary. The calendar was simple, easy to find since it was hanging on the wall next to the phone, and just the right size for all the orders—well, usually since business was increasing. Never the less, a determined Carl went one step further and had given her a set of books and writing utensils at Christmas to push her along toward becoming more professional in her record keeping. She expressed her thanks to him, but repeated that the bank calendar was fine with her.

This year's Savings & Loan calendar featured delicious looking desserts in each picture above the month's dates. Dollie paused for a moment to admire the beautiful dessert on display above her record book of pencil scratches. This month's dessert was a four layer chocolate cake with cherry sauce dribbling from between the layers. Every time she looked at the picture her mouth would water and she would think to herself, "I need to figure out how to make that."

Dollie leaned on the counter to get a closer look at the calendar. An item at a time she once again reviewed to make sure she had not forgotten something.

"Three pies?" questioned Dollie. "Humm....Banana Cream, Strawberry Rhubarb and—oh, yes, a Boston Cream Pie for Joyce Samucls. She picked it up earlier today. That's it!"

She stood erect and smiled. Nearly every day of the month there had been at least one order, but this week the calendar had been black with orders. With one hand she switched the overhead fan on and then turned it back off realizing it was still broken. Once again she mentally reminded herself to let Jack know about the fan.

Dollie eyed the pies and then the cupcakes still waiting to be topped and the cookies waiting to be boxed. With her finger she counted to make sure she had made enough for each order. She smelled the aroma of the banana bread and the pumpkin muffins. With a sigh of relief she looked at the clock and said aloud, "I'll ice the cupcakes when I get back. Now where did I put that list of items to pick up at the grocery store?"

Much of Dollie's success as a caterer was due to her neighbors and friends at church. For years Dollie had been delivering gifts of desserts or covered dishes to brighten the day of her friends and when her husband died and she found herself in financial trouble her neighbors started ordering baked goods to help her out. They insisted that she take money for them even though she wanted to do it for free. Eventually she began to accept the money and her business was started—Dollie's Catering Service.

Dollie had enjoyed preparing Sunday school parties or activities for her son's 4-H club. She had no idea that she had a knack for developing ideas and themes until she started getting invitations to put together receptions. She quickly became known for changing common events into special occasions. She knew the best recipes and decorations to have at an event whether a wedding party of 300 or a family dinner of ten.

Her continued success was in part because she was always looking for new ideas. Not satisfied to use the same recipes she sought to expand her inventory of recipes. Frequently on weekends she could be spotted at flea markets or auctions. She would be shoveling thru boxes and shelves of books looking for a unique or new recipe to use at the next event. Her collection of recipes included mostly Midwestern cuisine, but she was capable of featuring foods from several other cultures.

Rev. Jack Temple had grown close to the lady in the kitchen. She always had a scripture to quote, a word of encouragement, and a moment to bow her head for a prayer with him, but he was moved with emotion when she offered him a place to stay. The church parsonage had burned due to lightening striking it earlier in the year and Dollie immediately cleared out her store room and had an outside door installed for him to have an apartment there. He was overwhelmed with gratitude for her generosity. He had lost everything and this act of kindness helped him to get things back on track in a short time.

This Wednesday night seemed like any other Wednesday. At fifteen minutes before seven, the light went out in Dollie's kitchen as she covered the cookies and cupcakes, grabbed her purse and car keys and rushed out the door. She pulled a baseball cap out of her purse and pushed it down on her hair that desperately needed attention. She squirted a quick spritz of perfume across her to cover up any bad odors. She jumped into the driver's side of the car, slammed the car door, started the engine and quickly the sound of the motor of her blue 20 year old Plymouth could be heard as she hit reverse and moved backwards out of the garage and on to the street. Dollie glanced at her watch and nervously shifted into "drive" as she pressed the foot pedal down. Her tires squealed as the car jerked forward heading for the Nickerson Street Church.

For as long as Dollie could remember she had met at 7 p.m. Wednesday nights at the church for choir practice. Her mind was anticipating the new music that the group would be learning. There would be a discussion of plans for what the choir would sing at the upcoming Community Church Choir Competition. There would be plans made to meet the following Saturday afternoon at the local nursing home. There was a lot to decide and she didn't want to be late.

By the time she got two blocks to the four way stop— the only four way stop in town—she was speeding too fast to make a proper stop. There sat Officer Brown waiting for overzealous drivers who used Main Street to Nickerson Street as a race track. Dollie quickly applied her foot to the brake when she saw the officer.

"Screeeeeeeech!!" sounded the tires on the pavement.

The officer waved Dollie over and slowly walked to her window. He was smiling and shaking his head.

"Dollie," he began. "Where are you going so fast? You know you have to stop here?"

"Sorry Officer Brown," she began, "I was late leaving home for choir practice and I don't like to be late."

"If you had hit someone at that stop sign—and you might have since it appears you were not planning to stop until you saw me—well, I suspect the choir practice might have done without you for a long time—possibly forever. Now slow it down and get on your way and consider yourself warned."

Dollie breathed a sigh of relief. She nodded to him remembering what a nice student he had been in her Sunday school class 20 years earlier. He had grown into quite a fine man and was a dedicated policeman that most respected.

"God forgive me for my speeding, my being anxious about being late, my failure to always have the right attitude toward police. I know it was wrong to speed and I thank you for this man who stopped me before I had an accident. Thank you, Jesus for your watchful care. Amen"

Dollie turned into the parking lot at the Nickerson Street Church and was greeted by Emily Houseman. The two of them quickly walked together toward the church building's front entrance chatting about the unseasonable warmth for February.

Some in the congregation joked that the choir could not meet if it was not for Dollie. When she would hear such comments she would laugh back at them and deny it. She knew her voice was not solo material. She rated her voice right up there with the sound of "fingernails on the blackboard" and "hinges squeaking." Most disagreed with her assessment, but she kept her singing as a blend rather than a dominating influence in the sound of the choir.

Her humbleness was what made Dollie special. Everyone knew she was a supporter. She worked hard for the success of every project in the church but refused to be recognized or honored for it.

She didn't know how to direct the choir or play the piano or any other instrument. She had no part in organizing the choir or purchasing the music they used, but she was a regular, always present member, supporting the effort to provide enjoyable and inspirational music for the church.

The choir had also played a major part in the life of her husband while he was alive. In fact the two of them had met at a choir practice. Their son had become an active member when he was old enough and developed into a featured singer on many occasions. The choir was very special to her. Now that her husband had died and her son was married and living in Chicago she had grown closer to the choir. It had become her circle of friends and family.

As Dollie stepped into the foyer of the church she could hear the other choir members say, "Here she comes." Emily and Dollie made their way to the steps of the choir loft as the pianist began playing the vocal warm-up drills. "Ah" and "Ooo" could be heard echoing throughout the sanctuary as Dollie and Emily climbed the squeaky steps to the choir loft. With a deep breath the two reached the top step and laughed. The choir members were all turned toward the entrance to the loft looking at Dollie for an explanation of why she was late.

"Officer Brown and I were chatting," she said as a deep red blush came on her face.

The choir laughed a big laugh and not another word was necessary. The choir rehearsal began

CHAPTER TWO

Dollie had a lot of pride in the church choir as did all the choir members. If a bad performance occurred—and they did from time to time—the group of singers would gather early for practice to insure that the next Sunday's performance was a good one.

These "run of the mill" singers did remarkably well. Despite the fact that none of them had been professionally trained their enthusiasm and hard work along with the direction of Joan Stacy helped them to overcome any shortcomings in the area of vocal talent and provided the congregation with inspirational music each Sunday.

Director Joan Stacy was in her early 30's and still filled with lots of enthusiasm and energy for teaching and performing. In her movements as she directed you could sense how talented she was. She was able to draw emotion and excitement from the choir as she molded and shaped their sounds.

Individually, she was able to do a glorious performance of a selection from an opera as well as sing a pop song from the 50's and 60's. The choir loved to hear her sing and would encourage her to do so each rehearsal. When she performed a solo at church the congregation would stand applauding at the beauty of her performance.

The choir had become a wonderful public relations tool for Nickerson Street Church. Each month they performed at the local Sassafras Springs Assisted Living and Nursing Home. In the summer months, they presented community concerts in Grinstead Memorial City Park which is located directly across the street from the church. The group had a lot of fun sharing their music.

"Ca-ree-e-k!"

"Choir," began Joan, "let's start again at measure 54. Baritones need to sing out louder. You're getting lost when the sopranos go for those high notes. Soprano section, make sure you keep those notes on pitch. Don't pinch the sound."

The choir had been working on a couple of new compositions for the upcoming Community Church Choir Festival, but tonight Joan had distributed another new piece for the Sunday service. Colleen Marx commented early in the rehearsal that "Joan must have a lot of faith in the group passing this difficult number out."

Ignoring the comment, Joan turned to the organist and motioned to begin. It had been nearly an hour earlier they had started. No breaks were given the group as Joan pushed and encouraged and drove them to learn the song. The hard work was beginning to pay off as the piece did show signs of improving.

"Ca-ree-e-k!"

After nearly an hour of solid rehearsal the choir was beginning to stir. The sound of someone slowly coming up the stairs had their full attention and hope that it would bring the rehearsal to a temporary halt. The group noticeably needed a breather.

Joan Stacy had professional training at the local university and had sung professionally for a few years before she had become pregnant. Motherhood had pulled her out of the ranks of professional singers and into the house for duties of importance there. The love of performance had never left her though. The choir gave her a wonderful outlet to use her talent.

Joan's desire for perfection would sometimes cause her to forget she was working with volunteers who were not trained. She would push and push and drive the group to the performance level she wanted. Unfortunately she would stomp on a few toes and wear everyone out on the way.

When she first joined the choir she was the occasional soloist and Colleen Marx was the director. When Colleen became ill with the flu the previous year Joan stepped in to keep the choir singing. Everyone was excited to have her talent and immediately saw a marked improvement in the performances.

Joan knew the warm up drills. She knew how to pronounce the words so the listener could understand them. She shaped the harmonies into a beautiful blend. Her talent was unmistakable. The only problem was that she didn't know when she was pushing too hard.

On the other hand, the choir members were aware that they were gaining a reputation of being the best church choir in the community. They liked the attention they were getting. Joan had told them if they continued they would eventually get to host the Community Church Choir Festival. Most doubted that would ever happen as the two larger churches in town always had a connection that handed them the honor.

"Ca-re-e-ek!"

Some members of the choir began to squirm and shift from side to side as they wondered who was coming up the stairs. Located at the back of the choir loft, the person coming up the stairs could not be seen unless a choir member would turn around to see who was entering the loft. Joan, not wanting the distraction, worked to pull the choir's attention back to the front with instructions and increased the volume of her voice. Adding to Joan's frustration was Sherrie Bennett, the organist, who started stretching from her position to see who was climbing the stairs and was missing notes on the organ.

The stairs had become a humorous part of the history of the church building. There were many rumors about ghosts hiding underneath the stairs and making the steps squeak as someone would ascend them. Most thought that was silliness and reminded those saying such things that the old wooden steps had been there a hundred years and had held the choir members all that time. The stairs had good reason to squeak.

The church board considered replacing the steps at one point but the congregation voted not to as it was a part of the character of the building. The choir members had echoed the sentiment and stated they liked being able to hear someone coming up the stairs.

"Ca-re-re-e-eek!"

The curiosity to see who was coming up the stairs continued to grow. Despite the director's louder singing and frantic arm motions to keep the choir members on task, the singers began laying their music sheets aside in anticipation of the mystery person.

"Who could that be?" questioned Dollie. "It isn't any of the regular members of the choir. All are already here and in place."

Joan had high expectations and each Tuesday night she made a habit of phoning members to remind them of the rehearsal and to give them an idea of what would be covered in the meeting. Without fail, Joan would be at the church an hour early distributing copies of the music and insuring that everything was ready. She expected Sherrie Bennett to be there at least a half hour early so they could begin running thru the music. Joan was determined that every person get the most of their time at a rehearsal.

To hear someone coming in late was unusual. Dollie remembered being late one time and how embarrassing it was. She was thankful tonight that she made it right at the beginning and not any later. Without fail Joan would stare at the late comer from the front door to the stairs. A person could not see her while stepping up the stairs but the stare would be there when reaching the choir loft.

"Ca-re-e-ek" sounded the stairs again. This time Sherrie Bennett stopped playing and looked at the back. Joan dropped her arms to her sides and sighed. She quietly gave into the choir's desire to see who the mysterious stranger was. The sanctuary echoed with silence.

Below the choir loft, the sanctuary was completely dark. It gave a certain eerie feeling. The wooden beams in the vaulted ceiling gave the building an old world charm and the loft in the back was almost medieval in appearance. This architectural design allowed the choir to easily fill the auditorium with music. The sounds floated over the congregation on Sunday as though coming from the sky. Like angels, the choir would blend their sounds to make heavenly music, but now their silence left the building with a strange emptiness.

"Who is it?" Joan finally shouted out. "Who is coming up the stairs? You're late and costing us valuable rehearsal time."

"Ca-re-e-ek!"

The face of Rev. Jack Temple came into view.

"Sorry to interrupt," began the preacher. "I have an announcement. It just could not wait."

"What can be that important?" asked Joan. "Is the building on fire?"

"No, haha....not quite," replied Jack. "No, it is much more exciting than that."

"We were just about to start the special number for Sunday. It needs a lot of work," continued Joan as she glared at Rev. Temple.

"I don't think you will mind when you hear the news," continued Rev. Temple.

"We could use a break, Joan," said Margaret Cushing. "I don't remember working this hard in high school choir."

"Me neither," echoed Robert & Ralph, the Stewart twins.

"We'll stop for a while, but Rev. Temple, please make it quick. Now what is so important that you have interrupted our rehearsal?"

"I have just come from the Ministerial Alliance meeting at the Roland Park Baptist Church," Jack began.

Dollie could see that the longer Rev. Temple took to make the announcement the more frustrated Joan was getting.

Lord, give Joan the patience to wait and listen to Rev. Temple. She prayed.

Jack made his way to the front of the loft and joined Joan behind the director's stand. He took her hand and squeezed it shaking it with apparent pride.

"Tap, tap, tap," went Joan's foot on the floor. Rev. Temple placed his hand on her shoulder and turned toward the choir. His look was that of pride... like a proud father viewing for the first time his first born child. Then Rev. Temple took Joan and hugged her and said, "You did it!"

Rev. Temple's smile continued to get bigger. He looked at the choir members whose eyes were wide open. They had scooted to the edge of their seats. Their mouths were open with puzzled looks on their faces.

"You did it!" Rev. Temple repeated.

"Come on Rev," blurted out Margaret Cushing. "Don't keep us in suspense any longer!"

"What is it?" asked Colleen Marx. "Joan, do you know what he is talking about?"

Rev. Temple turned to Joan and said, "Do you think you can have five or six special selections ready by March 15?"

"Rev. Temple, you are skating on thin ice....What do you want?" replied Joan in a strong voice trying to get out of his embrace.

Dollie jumped up and said jokingly to the choir, "I better do something or we may see Rev. Temple being tossed over the balcony."

The choir laughed but went on buzzing with ideas of what Rev. Temple might be going to say. They continued asking each other questions. They buzzed with excitement sounding like a hive of bees circulating thru a beautiful flower garden. Finally, no longer able to control their excitement the choir members jumped to their feet and stared at Rev. Temple and Joan Stacy.

"Well," they said in unison.

They had never seen their minister this excited. This young unmarried handsome preacher had captured the hearts of the congregation with his enthusiasm and youthful energy. The young women had made a path from all directions to Jack's house bringing him every type of casserole dish or dessert. He didn't have to worry about food for several weeks thanks to the prospective brides.

"The Ministerial Alliance," began Jack, "has selected Nickerson Street Church to host the Community Church Choir Festival!"

Joan fell onto one of the pews in shock. The choir started cheering and jumping up and down causing the loft to shake. Each member was smiling wide.

"What did you say?" the choir said in unison.

"Yes," Jack continued. "We are going to host the choir festival. Right here in this building."

The choir began clapping loudly with their hands and stomping their feet. Echoes of the commotion came back to them as the entire building was filled.

"Hallelujah!" yelled Steve Elsea, the lead bass singer who ran the local hardware store.

"Fantastic!" hollered Jessica Blanden, the new hairstylist at the "Beau-ti-rama."

"Hurrah!" cheered others.

"The extra work the choir had done the past year in performing at various public events and at the area nursing homes got the attention of the neighboring churches," Rev. Temple continued.

Nickerson Street Church was smaller than several of the other congregations in the community, but the Alliance believed the Nickerson Street Church should host the Festival of Choirs just like the larger congregations if they were capable of performing such beautiful music. Joan had told the choir for a year in her pep talks and encouraging messages, "If you do your best and perform public service in the community, the choir will gain respect."

"Well, choir, here is your reward!" Rev. Temple announced.

The group turned and started applauding and cheering Joan. Dollie quieted the choir with a wave of her hand. "Thank you Joan for your hard work. We appreciate so much what you have done. We could not have done this without your encouragement, dedication and example as our director."

Joan continued to sit in the pew and frown. She rocked back and forth as though very upset. She twisted around looking at the floor and looked like she wanted to hide.

Dollie questioned in her mind, "What could be wrong with Joan at this moment of triumphant? This is a moment to be happy and joyful. This event was what Joan had hoped for all year. Every rehearsal she talked about how wonderful it would be to host the festival. She had encouraged the choir to work hard—to be good enough to host the festival. So here was the day—and so why is Joan upset? What could be wrong with Joan? Why was she not excited like the rest of the choir?"

"Joan," praised Colleen Marx. "We couldn't have done it without your constant encouragement. You were the one who reminded us at every practice that if we wanted to host the festival we would have to perform at our best."

"Thanks!" the whole choir shouted.

Dollie could see that even this compliment was not setting well.

Lord, help Joan with whatever problem she has. It must be a big one for her to be so depressed at such a happy time. And thank you for allowing us the opportunity to host the festival.

"We are going to host the festival," Dollie once again shouted.

Joan returned to the director's stand. She raised her hands to calm the choir. In a much more polite tone and forcing an artificial smile she called for order. Despite the smile, Joan still looked upset as she prepared to speak.

"Rev. Jack, we appreciate your coming to us with the news. We will certainly work hard to make you proud of us," she said

"Proud?" Jack responded. "I couldn't be prouder of you for bringing this honor to Nickerson Street Church. You have worked hard and this is your reward. The congregation has appreciated all of the specials this past year. In fact, the community has appreciated your extra efforts in witnessing to the shut-ins at Christmas when you went caroling over the town. The elderly have enjoyed your frequent visits to the nursing homes and hospitals. You have been a great example of Christ in this community. As the Scriptures says in Matthew 5:16, 'Let your light so shine before men, that they may see your good works and glorify your Father in heaven.'"

"We are pretty good," shouted Margaret Cushing, secretary at the Hathaway Insurance Agency.

"Yes, we are!" echoed the choir.

Joan looked even more dismayed. Dollie finally ignored Joan and became a part of the celebration. Joan always seemed to have some complaint or something negative in her view of things. Even in success she was depressed.

"Choir," began Joan while motioning for them to get quiet. "We have a lot of work to do if we are going to host the festival. We will need to practice every night this week. If Rev. Jack is going to announce that we are hosting the festival the congregation will expect us to sound particularly good this Sunday. Rev. Jack also said we would need five or six more songs. That is a lot for us to work on."

"We can do it," said Steve Elsea.

Joan gave Steve a dirty look, but continued, "We will need to set up a planning committee to organize various groups to operate such a big event. We don't just sing at these events. We have the refreshments, decorations, programs, advertising, etc. Do you see how much work that is going to be for me? This is not an honor—it's a lot of work!"

"Joan!" cried Colleen Marx. "You are ruining our moment."

"Well, let's get to work right now and sing through the song for Sunday's special. After that you can go back to celebrating," Joan sternly said wanting to get the rehearsal back on track.

"I can see that I should have waited until the end of the rehearsal," said Rev. Jack. "I should have known better. I'm sorry Joan."

"Never mind, what is done is done and now we need to focus," replied Joan.

Dollie winked at the minister as he was passing by on his way to the stairs. They had both talked about the dedication of Joan and her sometimes over dramatic reactions to events. He nodded with an understanding smile.

Thank you Lord for an understanding preacher who sees and understands our needs.

Sherrie cranked up the volume on the organ as the choir began singing. The surrounding neighborhood must have wondered what was going on at the church as the choir began to sing louder than ever before. Joan frowned.

"Stop!" cried Joan. "We aren't singing at the carnival. We don't have to sing a performance for the whole downtown now. Take a look at the message of this song. Do you think it should be sung loud or soft?"

"Sweet, sweet spirit," read Dollie. "Oh my, forgive us Lord. I doubt if God appreciated us shouting this beautiful song."

The choir began again in a much quieter tone, but Joan stopped them again. The sound being still too loud resulted in another pause to reflect on the words and message of the song. Joan looked around the choir. She pointed to Steve Elsea and asked him to sing the opening line as quietly as he could. He responded and the choir in unison sighed with comments at how beautiful it was. Joan then instructed Sarah Jenkins, a new soprano who had joined the choir a couple of weeks earlier to sing the same thing. Sarah responded beautifully.

"Now that is as quiet as I want you to sing," explained Joan.

"Joan, I would like to suggest that Steve and Sarah sing the opening. Maybe one sing and the other follow with the next phrase. Then the rest of us could join in," Dollie said.

"What?" said Joan as she was taken by surprise by the suggestion.

Dollie repeated her suggestion and Joan was suddenly smiling. "You do want to perform the best you can!" she exclaimed.

"Yes?" questioned the choir. "Of course we do. What do you mean with that comment?"

The choir members were confused with their director's reactions. They stared at her waiting for an explanation.

"I'm sorry," she began, "I should have been just as happy as you were about the invitation to host the festival. It is what I have wanted, but all I could think of was the work. I was afraid we could not do it the way it should be done. I didn't want to embarrass you or the congregation. I'm sorry. I see by Dollie's suggestion and the support you gave the idea that all of you do care about the choir and want the best. Thank you for being here tonight and every — —."

"Wait a minute?" broke in Lincoln Madison, a custodian at the local school. "You don't think we are good enough to host the festival, do you?"

"No," Joan quickly replied. "That's not it. I was afraid I wasn't good enough to prepare everything that needs to be done for the festival."

"You don't have to do everything," began Colleen. "We should divide the responsibilities with a director to oversee all of the planning. Joan, you have so much to do with the music and the programs — why don't we select someone else to be the director of the event and they can select committees to oversee specific needs of the festival?"

"Yes, that's a great idea," echoed the rest of the choir.

"Well, who would be willing to do it?" asked Joan. "I won't mind at all. It would be a great relief if I could just focus on the musical portion."

"Dollie," nominated Margaret Cushing.

"What?" responded Dollie thinking that Margaret wanted to ask her something and not realizing she was nominated for the director's job.

"Who better?' joined in Ralph and Robert Stewart. "All in favor say 'aye'?"

"Wait a minute!" moaned Dollie.

"Aye!" the choir shouted.

"Dollic is the director," said Joan. "Now let's get back to singing before she backs out."

CHAPTER THREE

Dollie was out of bed and in the kitchen pacing back and forth before sunrise. Her neighbor's cat, Charlie, scratched at the back door to get Dollie's attention. The cat knew it was time for their usual morning walk, but Dollie had other ideas. Dollie paced back and forth banging drawers and shuffling recipe books trying to overcome the nervous tension that had built up over night. The cat could be heard meowing loudly.

Dollie had taken care of Charlie several times for her neighbor when they would go on an overnight trip somewhere. This time it was a trip to the Final Four State Basketball Tournament. She enjoyed the cat and the two of them made it a regular event taking a walk each morning whether the cat was staying with her or not. They would meet at the back door. Today would be different as Dollie didn't have time for a walk.

"What was I thinking?" she thought as she contemplated how she was selected as director for the festival the night before.

"Dollie," hollered Rev. Jack Temple from his apartment. "Is that you making all that noise?"

Before Dollie could respond to Rev. Temple's questions the phone rang.

"Morning Dollie," the person on the phone said.

"Oh, hi Margaret," said Dollie into the phone.

"Dollie, I have some great ideas for the festival," began Margaret Cushing. "I'll meet you at the coffee shop in an hour."

"Oh Maggie, you have a lot of nerve calling me this morning after you got me in this mess. This is going to be a big job of being director. What were you thinking?"

"No one could do it better," continued Margaret, "You're a natural to be the director."

"I am a basket case this morning. I don't know where to begin," replied Dollie.

"Well, first you can meet me at the coffee shop in an hour. See you there," said Margaret as she hung up.

"Maggie, I can't— —Maggie? Are you there?"

It was too late. Margaret was gone and would be at the coffee shop in an hour like she said. Dollie would have to make arrangements for a walk later with the cat, but for now she needed to get on her way to deliver several baked items if she was going to get to the coffee shop on time.

Porter's Place, the local coffee shop in town was a special place. It had been the first bank in the town. For years Porter Conway was the president and when he died the bank was sold. The new owners immediately built a new building and moved out of the brick structure. Ike Winston, an innovative and historically minded individual got the idea of calling it "Porter's Place" in honor of Mr. Conway and featured coffee and pastries.

It was next door to Alice's Closet, a clothing store featuring vintage clothes. Margaret Cushing had taken the clothing store over when Alice found that she was needed at her daughter's home in Dayton, Ohio. Margaret was an excellent person to oversee it. She had a great ability to recognize clothing styles and was able to identify the decade they were worn. She also did an excellent job displaying the clothes in the store. Dollie enjoyed visiting the store and seeing the fascinating ways that Maggie would tell a story just by displaying clothes. A walk thru the store was like walking down memory lane.

Dollie quickly grabbed her hat and several boxes of baked goods and was on her way making deliveries and heading for Porter's Place. She started the car as she heard Jack in the kitchen saying, "Dollie, who was that on the phone? Dollie? Now where did you go?"

Rev. Jack Temple looked out the window in time to see Dollie fly by in her Plymouth waving.

"Now where is she going this time of day?" Jack said as he examined a couple of boxes of baked goods. "Hmmmm! Are these for breakfast?"

It was a short ride to the downtown after her last delivery was made. Dollie arrived just in time to see Ike Winston turn the sign from closed to open. Maggie was right behind her as they entered the store. Ike looked up surprised to see the two ladies coming in the store that early.

Ike was average height and a good looking man. He and his wife were known for making great soups and sandwiches at their first restaurant but when it was destroyed by a tornado a couple of years earlier the opportunity to purchase the bank came along and they took it. Despite being known as a coffee shop or Porter's Place it did have a lunch menu which included their delicious soups and sandwiches. It had become a favorite place for a lot of people in the community.

"Ladies," he greeted, "what are you doing here this early? I don't usually see you until mid-afternoon."

"You wouldn't believe Ike," answered Dollie. "This so called friend of mine got me into a big mess."

"Mess? Oh my, you two friends aren't fighting are you?" Ike asked.

"No," laughed Margaret," not at all. Dollie here is just a bit on edge because she is the director for the Community Church Choir Festival this year."

33

"Is she now," said Ike as he turned with a smile on his face. "And just how did you get that job? Surely Margaret didn't have something to do with that."

"Yes she did," began Dollie. "It was like a tsunami. I didn't know what hit me last night when the choir elected me. One minute I was rejoicing that Nickerson Street Church gets to host the festival and the next minute—SWOOSH! I'm swept into the leadership role."

"And a fine job you will do too," said Ike.

"See," said Margaret as she pointed her finger at Dollie. "That's just what I said, Ike. She is a natural for something like this. She will do a great job."

"Ok, enough… let's have some coffee. What kind of pastries do you have today? Something smells awfully good. I need some to get my strength," said Dollie in a better mood reflecting all the compliments that had been poured her way.

"I have a special new one," said Ike as he winked at Margaret. "I think it is just perfect for today. I'll be right back."

"What was I thinking? How could I leave choir practice last night with the idea that I could head up this whole event?"

"You'll do great! Just think of all the good feelings you will have knowing that you are doing something for the church," responded Margaret. "By the way, I made a list of some of the things you need to be planning."

"You what?" she asked with her eyes getting wider as she saw a lengthy list unrolling from Margaret's hand. "Ah, Maggie, it appears you should be the one in charge."

Reaching for her cell phone Dollie began to click in the numbers for the church.

"Hey, what are you doing?"

"I'm calling the church to resign and nominate you as director," replied Dollie.

"No you're not," said Margaret as she grabbed the phone.

"Ladies!!!" interrupted Ike as he set the coffee and two tarts in front of them.

"Wow, does that look good," pointed Margaret to distract Dollie from the phone.

"Ike, I don't know how you do it. These look delicious and they smell incredible."

"Dollie, you go ahead and enjoy the dessert. I think Margaret said she would pay for it today. Right Margaret?" eyeing her in an attempt to encourage making up for the disagreement between the ladies.

"Ok Ike.. I get your point and sure. Dollie, the breakfast is on me, but don't call and resign. I'll help you all I can, but you are the best person for the job."

"So, ladies, are you going on a buying trip today? That's usually the reason you are here early," inquired Ike.

"No, it has to do with the festival. I had some ideas and thought we could talk about them over coffee and your delicious pastry. Here, why don't you take a look at the list. See if you think I have left anything off," said Margaret as she handed it to Ike.

"Ike, this isn't raspberry....what is this?" asked Dollie with the fork in mid-air from tasting her first bite.

"You caught me," he laughed. "It's boysenberry."

"You're kidding. Where in the world did you get fresh boysenberries?"

"My secret....." Ike said winking and leaving the ladies without another word.

"Maggie, its February. Where in the world could he get boysenberries? Hummm. He never ceases to surprise me. This is delicious. Hurry up and take a bite and give me the list."

"List? I thought you had the list," Margaret said.

35

The two ladies heard the coffee shop door open and looked to see who was entering. There was Josh McDaniel, editor of the local newspaper. He waved at them and motioned for Ike to bring him coffee and the pastry of the day.

"Josh, good to see you again," said Dollie.

"Dollie, it has been too long," replied Josh. "I have been out of town. I was lecturing at the University the past month—Journalism classes. Rather fascinating to get to share with young minds preparing to become newspaper writers. What a lot of talented people!"

"That's good to hear," replied Dollie. "We could use a good editor for the local newspaper."

"Dollie!" laughed Margaret, "Don't insult our beloved editor Mr. McDaniel."

"So, who is going to tell me what you two are up to today," Josh said as he stared into their eyes to see if they were hiding something. "I know there is always a story when you two are around."

The two women laughed and tried to look innocent and like they had just met for a quiet breakfast together. Ike brought Josh's coffee and dessert and handed the list of ideas for the festival back to Margaret.

"I think you have a pretty good list of things to do. I would say you will finish around Christmas time," he jokingly commented.

"List?" pursued Josh knowing there was a story about to be shared. He reached for the list as Dollie quickly slid it away from his grasp. "Hope it is a good one as I have a spot on the front page."

Blushing Dollie turned to Margaret and said, "Maybe we should go. Don't want to be late for that sale."

"What sale?" said Margaret looking totally confused.

"You know? The sale at Alice's Closet? You are always getting ready for one and I'm here to help you."

"I'm not having a sale. What's wrong with you Dollie?" she said oblivious to Dollie's attempt to prevent Josh from hearing about the festival. "This being director of the Community Church Choir Festival is already stressing you out. Maybe someone else should take charge. I don't want my best friend getting senile—forgetful—empty headed."

"Maggie," said Dollie loudly with a raised eyebrow and looking in disbelief at Margaret for saying such a thing.

"Just joking," laughed Margaret.

"Festival director?" interrupted Josh. "So, it is true. I heard the Nickerson Street Church is hosting the event this year and it wouldn't take a nuclear scientist to guess that Dollie would be director. Who better?"

"Exactly!!!" said Margaret loudly in agreement.

"What did you people do? Rehearse this whole scene?" snapped Dollie.

"Josh, you apparently knew about this already? How did you find out? I thought it would be announced Sunday?" Margaret asked.

"The first time I heard it was last night when Officer Brown came by the newspaper office and told me. Said he had stopped Rev. Jack for speeding and while writing the ticket listened to him tell how proud he was and what an honor it was for the Nickerson Street Church to host the festival."

"Did you say Jack got a ticket? Hahaha. Wait until I get home," laughed Dollie.

"Yes, he did. Anyway, Officer Brown was eager to share the news and saw my light on at 2 a.m. He figured I needed company. Actually at 2 in the morning I don't need to be interrupted if I am working. Haha. But never the less he stopped by to share the news."

"You should have seen the reaction of Joan Stacy, our director," began Margaret. "You know her and how she always takes the negative side."

"Actually, I don't. I've never had the pleasure of meeting her. I'm not a member of your choir or church for that matter."

"Maggie, I don't think you need to share about Joan. Josh might put it in the n-e-w-s-p-a-p-e-r…." spelled Dollie.

"Like he doesn't know how to spell newspaper. Good one Dollie," laughed Margaret. "Your point is well taken, Josh. I guess you wouldn't know her."

"I just don't think it is necessary to share that. We should reflect on the positive side of the event. Seriously Josh, the choir was very excited and honored by the announcement. That is what you should put in the newspaper," urged Dollie.

"What made you think there would be something in the newspaper? Who cares about a bunch of church choirs getting together?" he joked.

"Josh! You—." Dollie cut her comment short realizing he was tormenting her. He often did that. The two of them had become good friends over the years. Josh and she had been childhood sweethearts, but during junior high her parents moved away to a neighboring town for a year. When she returned a year later Josh had been sent to California to live with his grandparents. The two of them renewed their friendship a few years ago when Josh returned to operate the local newspaper.

"Is the choir getting new robes for the occasion?" guessed Josh. "Is that why you two women are meeting here today—to plan a fundraiser?"

"Robes? Ha-ha…ah..,er…new robes?" paused Dollie and Margaret looking at each other.

"It just seemed like something you two would want for such a special occasion and with Margaret's connections in the fabric industry that should make it easy to arrange. Probably get a good price."

"Robes? I like the idea," thought Margaret. "What do you think Dollie?"

"Bad time of year to ask for donations. I don't think the church could afford them right now. It would be nice though and we do need them. The choir robe I wore Sunday had a worn place in the back where I was to sit down. Thought at the time it looked pretty shabby."

"True, we do need them. How about someone donating the entire amount? Who do we know that could do that?" asked Margaret.

"Frankly, what we really need is air conditioning. If we get that big crowd in our building in March it will be sweltering," commented Dollie.

"Oh yes, Dollie!" exclaimed Margaret. "You are right about that. We have to do something. Say, what if we have the festival in the park across the street? Then we could focus on buying robes and the need for air conditioning would be eliminated for the time being?"

"Say, Josh, don't suppose you would like to donate a few thousand dollars so we could buy those robes right away? So how about it?" said Dollie looking directly at Josh.

Taking his wallet out of his back pocket, he said, "Here's $25 to start you off. Afraid I can't do much more than that."

"I've got it!" interrupted Margaret. "We can have a sale in the church. Get people to donate items and then have a big garage sale. We could make a lot of money doing that. Might have a meal of some sort at the same time. Spaghetti or chili."

"Wait a minute," broke in Dollie, "we haven't decided to buy robes and we don't have the authority to launch a big fundraiser. The church board needs to be contacted."

"Ask Rev. Jack when you get home," responded Margaret.

"From what I saw last night it shouldn't be difficult to get him on board to support getting new robes," encouraged

Josh. "He was very proud of the choir according to Officer Brown."

"Ok, I'll do it," said Dollie. "As soon as he comes in this afternoon I'll talk to him about buying robes and that we are ready to have a fundraiser to make it happen."

"Good," shouted Margaret. "I'm off to tell the Stewart twins and Colleen to start spreading the word that people can bring items to the church building."

"Hey, we need to get it approved first," said Dollie as Margaret was heading for the door.

"I'll put something in the newspaper encouraging people to bring items to the church," said Josh as he made his way for the door. "That should get some things coming from others in the community who don't attend Nickerson Street Church."

"Great idea, Josh," said Margaret as she opened the door. "That's very nice of you."

"Anything to help out my favorite two ladies," laughed Josh.

"Hey," shouted Dollie, "hold up there. We need to at least talk to the choir. They may not even want robes. Wait a minute."

It was hopeless to stop the two as they rushed out the door on a mission to round up support to buy robes. Deserted, Dollie looked down at Maggie's list of things to do. The six pages of notes must have covered every possible problem and need that the festival could possibly have. She had a deep sinking feeling inside her stomach as she considered the magnitude of this new venture.

Lord, give me the strength and patience to do this job. Help me to know what to do and who to appoint for the various positions on the committees. Help me to always keep focused on you, Lord... This is for you and not for the glory of Nickerson Street Church, the choir or any individuals. Let us shine with the message you want us to share.

As she raised her head from praying she heard the two familiar voices of Robert and Ralph Stewart. They were dressed in matching blue sweaters with a snowflake design and gray pants. One wore loafers and the other lace shoes. Robert always wore loafers and Ralph laced shoes. It had been that way since Junior High School. They were identical in appearance and the shoes were the only way to identify which was which.

"Marge said we were going to have a garage sale to raise funds to buy new robes," began Ralph. "About time we got robes. That one I had on Sunday was taped together with duct tape in back."

"You're kidding," laughed Dollie. "Are you serious?"

"Well, actually no, but if I had some I would have repaired it with duct tape. I held it together to keep it from falling off of me."

"How was yours, Robert?" Dollie asked as she turned to the twin brother.

"Mine was ok. Certainly better than Ralph's. When Maggie mentioned the idea of a supper Ralph and I volunteered to oversee a chili supper. Hope you don't think that is silly."

"Not at all," replied Dollie. "What led you to do that?"

"We bought a half a beef not realizing how much meat that is and need to get rid of a lot of it. What better way than providing it for the church to raise money?" replied Ralph.

"Excellent! Are you donating the meat or will we need to pay you?" asked Dollie.

"We are donating it.," the two men said at the same time.

"Besides," continued Robert," we have this great chili recipe we got from friends in Minnesota. It takes brown sugar and ground mustard. You'll love it."

"Wow! Things are moving along so fast. I can't keep up. So what do I do?" asked Dollie.

"Nothing," replied the Stewart twins in unison. "We know you have a lot to do so we are happy to take charge of this part to help you out. Of course we will contact you and keep you aware of the plans. You concentrate on the other things."

"Thanks guys...that is very nice of you and I must say looking over this list of things that Maggie has for us to do I can use a lot of help."

"Dollie," Ike called, "It's Rev. Jack on the phone. He wants to know if you are going to be home for dinner."

"I'll take the call if that is alright," she responded. "I need to apologize to him for running out before breakfast this morning. I don't think I left a thing in the house for him to eat——oh my, except for the Jackson birthday cupcakes... oh my."

Dollie took the phone from Ike's hand and began talking, "Jack, did you find anything to eat for breakfast? Cupcakes? Noooo.. You didn't?"

Jack reassured her that he had not eaten the cupcakes despite admiring them and looking them over rather closely. Dollie looked a little pale as she realized she had forgotten to deliver the cupcakes for the birthday party scheduled that afternoon. She quickly grabbed her purse and started to say "good by" to Jack when he interrupted.

"I ate peanut butter sandwiches so don't worry about me," he continued. "Dollie, your son called. He wants to know if you are still coming to Chicago to visit him."

"Oh, my," she exclaimed. "I forgot about our plans and that is the same week we have scheduled the choir competition!"

"Well, that won't work," replied Rev. Temple. "You have to be here. We can't do it without you. Do you want me to deliver the cupcakes for you? Who did you say they were for? I don't mind."

"Would you?" she asked Rev. Temple. "That would help a lot. You are a god-send."

Dollie grabbed her purse and bid farewell to Rev. Temple as she hung up the phone and moved toward the door of the restaurant. She waved to Ike as she tossed some money on the table and said she had to go and wished him a great day. She glanced at the long list she had gotten from Maggie.

"How will I get all of this done?" she wondered.

CHAPTER FOUR

D riving back from Porter's Place, Dollie took a slight detour into the Sassafras Springs Cemetery. She occasionally would visit her husband's grave—especially when life seemed a little too tough or she felt alone. Howard Burgess had been a special husband and their relationship was quite close. His death had been a blow to her, but she loved him now as much as ever.

"The people that mowed the cemetery did a commendable job," she thought as she drove in the entrance. "Did I put those pruning shears in the trunk? I need to trim just a little grass from around the stone."

In her view, there was always a little grass around the stone that needed to be trimmed. Cutting those little sprigs of grass was her way of doing something for Howard. It also allowed her an opportunity to talk over a few things while working. She missed him. Since he had been gone nothing seemed as enjoyable or fulfilling. There was always an emptiness.

She pulled the car beside the redbud tree at the edge of the north road of the cemetery which put her just a few steps away from Howard's grave. The view was beautiful from this part of the cemetery. Some caring people had planted a collection of spring blooming bulbs in a cluster at the base of the redbud tree. The crocus were in full bloom. It was a welcoming sight to Dollie.

"Howard," she began. "Do you see those beautiful flowers? This is a peaceful place."

"Mrs. Burgess?" interrupted a voice behind her.

"Oh?" she exclaimed with surprise. "Who is it? Oh, Chuck, what brings you here?"

"I saw you over here and wanted to thank you again for dropping by all that food last week," he replied.

"Not a problem, Chuck," she began as she remembered that Chuck's mother had died the previous week. "I was so sorry to hear about your mother. Mrs. Stein was a nice woman. She helped me in several events for the 4-H program. It's hard to say good by to a loved one. I can imagine you miss her a lot. I still miss my husband, Howard. I come here about once a month to talk to him."

She motioned with her hand toward her husband's grave. "I come and trim around the stone. Sometimes I bring flowers and sometimes I just come and sit. Don't say a word. I just sit to feel close to him."

"Mr. Burgess....Now that was a fine man," Chuck began. "I never told you this, but he caught me smoking down by the church one night. Scared me to death. He grabbed me by the collar of my shirt and shook me. Then just as quickly he let me loose and told me how his father died of lung cancer."

"Howard shook you? That must have been quite a sight. Did your friends see it?" asked Dollie knowing that some of Chuck's friends were known as pretty tough characters.

"No," he continued. "I think that is what scared me the most. I was standing there alone when this big guy came up and shook me."

"His father died from cancer directly related to smoking. Howard rarely talked about it with me. He never got over losing his father in such a painful way. Howard would drive to Chicago to the Cancer Research Center each night. We lived about 2 hours from Chicago then. That was before we moved back to Sassafras Springs."

"Two hours one way?" asked Chuck.

"Yes," continued Dollie. "Howard would leave work and go directly there. It was hard on our relationship, but I did understand. I knew how much he loved his father. The day Howard came home earlier than usual—well, I knew it was over. All over his face was grief. Mr. Burgess is buried right over here. Now Howard is buried here."

"Your Mr. Burgess was a very sincere man. He really tried to get me to quit smoking. I haven't quit completely, but he made me stop and think about it. Seeing you here reminded me about Mr. Burgess. I watched him live his life after that. I saw him work with the Little League in coaching and knew of his support for the Boy Scouts every time they had a fund raiser. The man was a saint."

"I always thought so. I have often wondered if he was a wild kid when he was younger. I didn't get to know him until he was grown. For as long as I have known him he has been dedicated to helping young people whenever he could."

"Say, I heard that Nickerson Street Church is hosting the choir festival this year and that you are directing the whole thing." inquired Chuck.

"They asked me to be the festival director and I don't know what I was thinking. What a job!" she gasped.

"I bet. Did you accept?"

"I'm not sure."

"How does that work? You accepted or you didn't. Can't be both ways," questioned Chuck.

"I'm not sure I said yes. I heard my name called. I asked a question of what they wanted. Next thing I know they voted and I was in. The choir disappeared so fast I didn't have a chance to decline the invitation."

"Ha-ha," laughed Chuck.

"That will teach me to do a little less talking and to be more observant of what is going on around me," she chuckled.

"Who could do a better job?" Chuck encouraged.

"You're a nice man to say that, but the amount of work— I won't have time for my catering business."

"Sure you will. You'll work it out. If you have something you think I could do, let me know. I'll be there. Don't go to church much, but for you—I'll do it. Good to see you, but I better get back home," he said as he hurried off to meet some friends at the east gate of the cemetery.

"So, Howard, what do you think?" she said as she sat down next to Howard's tombstone and began clipping grass. "Did I bite off more than I can handle?"

A breeze started to blow against her face in a warm embracing way. She imagined that it was Howard hugging her. It was like he was giving her an encouraging warmth of confidence that she could do the task ahead. She always felt that he was with her no matter what the problem or challenge.

Rev. Temple had said he felt his mother's presence that same way. Others of Dollie's friends had said similar things about their loved ones. It was reassuring to know that her Howard was close by.

Turning toward her car she took one last glance toward the tombstone and motioned a kiss good bye. She needed to be on her way if she was going to be ready for the meeting at the church that night.

As she got into her car the verse of Scripture came to mind, "I can do all things thru Christ who strengthens me." This brought a smile to her face. She had her answer.

"Exactly," she thought. "Who can be against us if God is for us? Let's get to the work before us."

CHAPTER FIVE

At 5 p.m., Dollie raced down the street in her car; rolled into the Church parking lot; and came to a screeching halt. She was determined to get a head start on the planning by displaying a chart of available jobs and committees before anyone else arrived.

As she opened the car door she was welcomed with applause from people already working in the yard. Jerking her neck to see what was happening she was stunned to see several already present for the meeting. Her plan to arrive an hour before everyone was not going to be a reality. She was looking like she was late with the crowd already assembled. Her neck and shoulders began to tighten.

There was Mark Miller mowing the front yard. Robert and Ralph were carrying containers of soup and other foods. Angie Simpson was planting flowers around the front church sign. Rev. Temple was raking a portion of the churchyard and giving instructions to a man she had never seen before. He was helping with new shrubbery. She noticed he had the emblem of the local Greenhouse on his shirt.

"Dollie," shouted Rev. Temple. "See the new shrubbery the local greenhouse has donated to the church."

"Donated? That's wonderful," she replied.

"Need some help?" asked Josh McDowell, editor of the local newspaper as he came up the walk.

"You're here too?" replied the surprised Dollie.

"I brought this desk over from your house. Rev. Temple said he didn't have room for it so thought he would donate it for the garage sale."

"That is so nice of him. I think that was the only thing he saved when his house burned," Dollie commented.

"I thought I recognized it," said Josh. "I remember him dragging it out of the house and our having to hold him back from going in again. That was a terrible day. Always terrible when someone loses their things like that."

"Yes, it was awful."

"And like usual, you took the initiative and made a place for him to live," said Josh with an admiring tone. "You have to be one of the finest ladies I know. Always helping and always caring about those around you."

"Hey, none of that," she told him with redness coming to her cheeks.

"Anything I can do?" he asked again.

"Here, you can help me take this display in the building. I want to set it up in the dining hall so people can get a good look at the various committees."

"If you let me have one of those cookies, you can consider the display on its way."

"It's a deal," she laughed.

As Josh and Dollie entered the building, Dollie came to a complete halt. For a moment she just took in the entire view of the sanctuary. She could hear voices in all directions and many were voices of people she did not know. Some were working on polishing the pews and washing windows. Others were on ladders replacing bulbs in the light fixtures. Rugs were being cleaned with shampooers. All of these jobs were on her list to assign. She had worked all day organizing everything, but it appeared that everything would get done before she had a chance to assign jobs.

Thank you Lord for these wonderful volunteers. They make the job much easier. And thank you for your providing them with this enthusiasm that is spreading to others.

During the afternoon, Dollie had been to the school supply store to get materials; obtained prices from the printers for making posters and invitations; stopped at home to get the cookies she had promised Robert and Ralph; and looked around the house for a few items to bring for the garage sale. Yet in all this rushing and working to be an hour early she was one of the last to arrive.

"What an example I am," Dollie said in frustration.

"Hey, Dollie," shouted Colleen from across the room. "I called a few people in the church and encouraged them to gather some things for the garage sale, but I had no idea we would get this kind of response. Isn't this great?"

Colleen had done a remarkable job contacting the church members. She had asked the members to contact their neighbors and friends for items for the sale. The effort began to snowball as more and more people decided to help the congregation that had provided encouragement and support during various times of trouble or need. Numerous boxes filled with items for the garage sale were being unloaded from trucks and vans.

Dollie worked her way back thru the rapidly filling room to return to her car. There were books, clothes, nice pieces of furniture, and even contributions from various businesses. She spotted a cookbook, an apron, a tray—all of which she could use in her business.

"The items I brought for the garage sale won't add much," she thought.

She stepped out of the door just in time to see Chuck carrying a large container of flowers around the side of the building. He backed up and shouted to her.

"Hey, Mrs. Burgess!" Chuck greeted. "I said I would stop by. Wasn't here a minute before Rev. Temple had me working. How about that one?"

"What are you going to do with those beautiful flowers?" remarked Dollie admiring the huge blooms on the plants.

"Follow me and you'll see." Chuck replied with a certain sense of pride.

Dollie followed Chuck around the corner of the church building and found a group busily working on making a few new flower beds. Additional shrubs had been placed at the side of the entrance. Two other men were painting the church sign and another was up a new pole in the parking lot installing an outside light.

"Wow, even the Feed the Children project didn't get this much attention and support. This is incredible," Dollie said beaming with a huge smile as she returned to the dining area and met Colleen.

There was Lincoln Madison carrying a pair of leather chairs into the room. Dollie decided she would buy one of those chairs for Rev. Temple to use in his apartment. He had only an old worn out rocker she had brought down from the attic to use and this would be much more comfortable.

Next to Colleen was Mildred McKenzy sorting thru a box of nice clothes donated by Dollie's neighbor, Julia Ferguson. Going down the line she could see Georgia Maples unloading and sorting a box of vases. At another table on the other side of the room was Cora Smith. This caught Dollie's eye as she had long wanted a knitted sweater from Cora Smith, considered to be one of the finest knitters in the state. She had won many grand champion ribbons and awards at the State Fair.

On the other side of the room was Sarah Jenkins unwrapping a set of dishes she had brought. Doing a quick count, Dollie found there were some thirteen other women unwrapping or unloading items from boxes in the room. At the entrance to the multipurpose room Gunther Rapp was

unloading bags of dog food donated by the town veteri-
narian for the sale. There was Officer Brown wheeling in a
couple of bicycles the city had found abandoned in the park
the previous year. Officer Brown thought it was time for the
bikes to be moved out of the storage room at the jail.

Jason Granby, Dollie's neighbor across the street, entered
with a box of items. She was startled to see him there as he
wasn't a member of the Nickerson Street Church. Although
they got along as neighbors most of the time, they had never
been close. She strained to see what he had in the box. Seeing
the contents made her have a lump in her throat.

Jason had brought a box of pet toys that he no longer
needed since his pet terrier had been sent back to the farm.
Dollie remembered that wonderful day when the terrier was
returned. She and Rev. Temple had dealt with the "yelping"
for weeks and then there was the matter of having to watch
where they stepped when they left the house. It was truly
a day of celebration when they found the dog was leaving.
Now she felt a bit guilty as she knew how much the dog
meant to Jason and to see his generosity now in donating the
items made her feel closer to the man.

She watched him for a minute as he looked more and
more depressed with each toy he removed from the box. She
couldn't stand it any longer and finally went over and thanked
him for the wonderful contribution and then asked how the
dog was doing back at the farm. She added how much more
enjoyable it must be for the dog to be able to run free.

Looking over the room again, Dollie marveled at what
had been assembled in such a short time. With the sale
another day away she wondered if more things would be
brought during the final day before the sale. There wasn't
much room left and she was wondering where more items
would be placed. Then she panicked thinking if everyone
donated who would buy the items? What if everything is
left? What would the church do with everything?

Lord, thank you for opening people's hearts to provide this abundance of merchandise. Now send buyers so that our work will be blessed.

Colleen Marx was busily placing prices on items with Joan Stacy arranging the items on another table next to the sanctuary door. Everyone was so busy that few took time to greet Dollie as she toured the room. She felt a little lost among the workers.

"No matter," she thought and immediately went to work setting up the poster boards she had prepared. On each sheet was the title of a committee and a place for the names of the members and their responsibilities. She had thought it would be a long meeting and difficult to find enough volunteers to fill the committees. Now with many of the tasks already completed it might not be as difficult as she had thought.

"Dollie," shouted Colleen. "Come over here. I want you to see these teddy bears."

"Teddy bears? Now what was Colleen thinking?" wondered Dollie.

"Aren't these the most adorable things you have ever seen. They were used at the Weinberg's wedding a couple of months ago. Remember?"

"Colleen—I don't have time—" began Dollie.

"Look at them Dollie."

"What?"

"Can't you see them with choir robes on instead of a tuxedo and bridal gown? They would be perfect for the centerpiece at the refreshment table for the choir festival," Colleen insisted. She placed a piece of material on one and adjusted to make it look like a choir robe. "See?"

"Ok? Maybe?" replied Dollie, looking at Colleen with a questionable expression.

"Seriously," insisted Colleen in a stronger voice. "You don't remember them do you?"

"I did most of the refreshments and catered the rehearsal dinner, but I was busy in the kitchen preparing food when the couple cut the wedding cake. I really don't remember seeing them," admitted Dollie.

"Then you don't know what they do." Colleen continued.

"Do?"

"Didn't you do the decorations for the cake table?" continued Colleen.

"No, Julie's aunt did the wedding cake table. She told me she had something special——ah, the bears!" said Dollie.

"Well, let me show you what they do," said Colleen as she reached to click a switch on the bears.

The teddy bears started vibrating back and forth and moved around in a circle as though dancing. Dollie nodded that she thought they were cute. Then Dollie's eyes lit up as the two bears begin to sing "All You Need Is Love." One bear had written on it "Peace" and the other "Love."

"You know, Colleen," began Dollie, "these bears would be perfect for the choir festival."

"Oh really?" said Colleen in a mocking tone just as the two of them burst out laughing.

"Can you imagine anything better that this for the main table of food? They are adorable," continued Colleen.

"The only problem I have with them is that they might take a lot of room from the food?" commented Dollie.

"All you need is love," sang along Colleen.

"They are cute bears and the song is appropriate," began Dollie as she studied the two dancing bears. "They could be a real hit. I like the 'Peace' and 'Love' on them as well."

"Here is another idea," continued Colleen. "That could be the theme of the festival, 'Let us have peace and love in our community.' What do you think?"

"Now you are talking," agreed Dollie. "I like it."

"Ah, you see my vision for the bears. Good. We can't let these sell. Where should we put them?"

"How about in the closet here by the door to the sanctuary? Colleen, don't let me forget to take them home tonight. You know, the more I think about it the more I like the idea. This is great."

"I won't forget to tell you," Colleen said as she placed the bears in the closet.

Dollie returned to the multipurpose room where more items had been stacked and were waiting to be priced. She picked up a marker and tags and started pricing the items as fast as she could. She was making good progress until she heard the familiar voice of Josh. She wondered what he was back for this time.

Looking his direction she saw he was bringing in a beautiful old library table. She stopped writing and raised her head to take another look. That table looked familiar to her.

"Josh, where did that table come from?" she shouted.

"Ah, well, your uncle donated it," he answered with a look on his face as though he was the cat that had swallowed the canary. He was up to something.

"But, ah….that's my table," she paused.

"What was it doing at your uncle's house?" Josh asked.

"I loaned it to him because I didn't have a place for it. He must have forgot."

"Then should I take it to your house?" asked Josh.

"No," sighed Dollie. "I don't have any place for it either. Guess selling it and letting the money go for choir robes would be alright."

She ran her fingers along the top and remembered sitting underneath it Sunday afternoons at her grandparents. She had a lot of fond memories suddenly filling her mind and all because of a table. She remembered how the sides of the table were bookcases and her reading books were stored there. She also placed coloring books and her box of crayons.

"Well, the memories are still here," she said as she tapped the side of her head. "Time to let go of the table. You can't keep everything....but I sure did hope to have that table in the front room with a bouquet of fresh tulips for Easter like Grandma used to have."

"I can take it to your house," interrupted Josh when he heard her mumbling about tulips.

"Oh, did I say that out loud? Sorry," she responded.

More and more church people continued to come to help the choir members. There were so many people that Dollie began to wonder how Robert and Ralph were doing in the kitchen preparing food for this huge crowd. She slipped into the kitchen area and was surprised to see the counters burdened with sandwiches and salads, pies and cakes along with the bubbling chili on the stove. Ralph and Robert were busily cutting pies and cakes but immediately stopped and looked at Dollie.

"Do you see all of this food?" said the twins in unison.

"Yes, I do. I can't believe you have been able to prepare all of this in such a short time."

"We didn't," they responded. "Ike Winston sent over 6 dozen sandwiches from his shop and a dozen pies. Then others started bringing food as well. How many people are out there anyway? There must be the whole town."

"Not quite," said Dollie. "There are a lot and they will thoroughly enjoy this meal. Are you about ready?"

Dollie went into the multipurpose room and called for the people to get everyone in the dining hall for the meal. The group quickly assembled themselves and quieted in anticipation of the prayer.

"What would we do without the love of God? He fulfills our needs even when we don't know we need something," shared Dollie as she thanked God again. "Friends and neighbors, may I have your attention? Please convey our thanks to Ike Winston for donating the sandwiches and many of the pies. Also give a hand for Ralph and Robert who prepared the wonderfully delicious chili and oversaw the preparation of this meal."

The crowd cheered and clapped a big ovation. Ralph and Robert bowed and waved to the crowd. They were excited that they were able to do something for the church.

"Also," continued Dollie, "thanks to all of you who have donated items for the sale; worked in cleaning the building and repaired things that needed attention. It is a joy to see all the lights working and not one burned out."

She was interrupted with applause at that announcement. They all cheered again at the beautiful job being done. She went on praising the group and thanking God for everyone there. Then she called on Rev. Temple to have the blessing for the meal.

"Our Father, bless this work that is being done in preparation for the choir festival that we might continue to be a witness in the community. Bless each one's effort. Guide each of us as we seek to do your will. Especially at this time we pray thanking you for the bountiful meal prepared and provided for us. May the meal refresh our bodies, the fellowship feed our souls, and your Spirit guide us. In your son's name we pray, Amen."

"Ching-ching!"

"What was that?" said Dollie as she handed out plates. "Maggie, did you hear that noise? Sounded like a chain rattling."

"Hear what?"

"That strange noise. It was like—I don't know. Ah? Never mind. Let's eat," said Dollie as she turned her attention toward the meal.

CHAPTER SIX

Following the meeting, Dollie was pleased and relieved that people had volunteered so quickly for the various committees. Not a position was left unfilled. She gathered her things to leave the church building. As she stepped to the door she could hear voices in the parking lot as the committees were making plans to meet the following night.

"This is unbelievable. These people are an example to the world," Dollie thought.

She had always been proud of the little congregation, but tonight she was deeply impressed with their commitment. "Surely, God would bless their efforts," stated Dollie. "This will be one of the best choir festivals ever. What a great faith in God they have."

Dollie took hold of the doorknob and continued. "When I get home I must call Uncle John and thank him for donating the table. I guess it was really his to give away since I had no use for it and gave it to him."

Thank you, Lord, for allowing me to be a part of such a wonderful group of Christian people. Their faith is unquestionable.

Before she shut the lights off, Dollie turned and looked at the tables burdened with items for the sale. She walked into the sanctuary and examined the freshly polished pews and glimmering light fixtures. She could not remember things ever looking this clean and nice. She opened the side door and looked at the freshly planted flower garden and new shrubs. Everything was perfect. She returned to the door that led to the parking lot. By this time the voices had disappeared and darkness and silence began to surround her.

Dollie opened the entry door and stepped out into the night air. She felt a feeling of being lifted to heaven for a second. She felt so close to God at this moment. The excitement of the evening gave her chills. She was not yet ready to go home, but checking her watch she realized that it was late. Despite the hour she wanted to keep talking with someone about the meeting and making plans for the festival. She wanted the evening to continue.

"Going to a friend's house at this hour is totally out of the question," she thought. With a sigh and a laugh she flicked the lights off in the sanctuary. "Uncle John, wonder if he is up? He would enjoy hearing about this and I do want to talk about that table?"

"Cling-ching!" came a soft sound in the sanctuary as Dollie released the doorknob and the door shut with a thud.

"What was that?" she said as she recognized that same sound she had heard a few hours before. She took the doorknob and tried to open the door. It was locked.

"Well, of course it is locked, Dollie Burgess. You were locking it," she laughed. "We'll check for noises tomorrow since you don't have your key to unlock it."

She looked around and suddenly the feelings of spiritual celebration of the evening were being replaced with an uneasiness. She suddenly realized she was alone in the parking lot and there was no light. There was a sound in the bushes and the warm breeze had quickly turned to a cool breeze. She felt a slight mist on her face.

"I better get home," she decided looking around at the deserted street.

As she closed the door on her old blue Plymouth her mind wondered what she had heard. She tried to pinpoint where the noise was coming from but she couldn't. She thought to herself, "It sounded like it was in another room every time."

She started the car and placed it in gear just as her foot slammed on the brake. She was horrified. "What if it is the oven or that old coffee percolator? Or the heating system shorting out? We could have a fire and the entire church!! All these donations!!! I've got to get a key and find out what the noise is."

She pulled on to the street and headed home. On her way she noticed that Colleen had a light so she pulled in to her driveway. Jumped out and ran to the door and rang the doorbell. When no one answered the door she looked in the window to see if anyone was home. There was a light, but she didn't hear or see anyone moving around. She pounded on the door. Suddenly she found herself getting a bit panicked.

"Where was Colleen? She should be home now."

Dollie shrugged her shoulders with a puzzled look. The mysterious noise would not be solved tonight unless she drove home and got her own key and then went back to the church building. The thought of driving into the deserted parking lot in the dark and then having to get out of the car by herself seemed rather stupid at this moment as large rain drops began to fall.

"Ok, Lord," she prayed, "it is in your hands. I trust the building is safe and that the noise will wait until tomorrow."

Dollie turned her mind to other matters and began listing things that had to be done the next day. She would need to stop by Ike's to let him know how much everyone appreciated the sandwiches and pies. She must get the posters printed and the invitations must be addressed and mailed. Dollie stopped the car and reached for a pencil and pad to write the items down as she knew she would forget something if she didn't.

She felt a breeze blow around her like she had felt in the cemetery. Her mind thought of Howard once again. She thought about how proud he would have been to see all those volunteers working. They were all giving of their time and sharing what they had. It was a very good night. She was overcome with a desire to sing.

"Bless be the tie that binds, our hearts in Christian love—"

"Tap-tap-tap," came a sound on the window.

Dollie nearly had a heart attack right there as she jerked her head toward the window to see what it was. There stood Officer Brown with a flashlight in hand.

"Are you alright?" he asked. "Little late for you to be parked by the side of the road. Car working ok?"

"Oh yes," she laughed. "Just stopped to make a list while it was fresh in my mind. This choir festival is going to be the end of me yet. Besides, it isn't that late. What is it? Ah, just 9 p.m."

"Cold front is moving in and expecting storms tonight so you better get home right soon, Mrs. Burgess. You take care. I'll follow you home to make sure you are safe."

"Officer Brown, it isn't that late, but I do appreciate your help. That is very nice of you," Dollie said.

Officer Brown finally was persuaded that she was alright and wouldn't need an escort home. He drove off just as Dollie put the car in gear and rolled back on to the main road and headed home.

"Now, where was I," she questioned. "That was nice of Officer Brown, especially after I was speeding and nearly went thru the 4-way stop last night. Hummm. Now where was I? Oh yes, what was that sound?"

She drove in her driveway and remained in the car contemplating the sound. She wondered if it could be something in the kitchen that needed to be turned off. She had checked everything—she thought. Maybe it was the speaker system? No, they had not used it so it would not have been on. It was nothing outside and the sanctuary looked wonderful with all the light fixtures repaired and polished.

"This mystery will have to wait until tomorrow because this woman is going to bed. There is a lot to do and I need a good night's sleep to deal with it all," she said aloud as she opened the door of the car.

She gathered her things and got out of the car just in time to bump heads with Rev. Jack Temple who had come to see what was taking her so long to get home.

"Ouch," said Dollie. "Jack, what are you doing out here?"

"I was worrying about you," he answered. "The meeting was over for some time and I thought you would be home by now. Are you ok?"

"What is this? Do I look like an old woman wandering around needing help?"

"Oh no," he laughed, "of course not. You do better than anyone I know that is your age."

"My age?" she said as she raised an eyebrow showing her annoyance with that comment.

"Now Dollie, don't you go twisting my words. You know very well I was concerned about you as a fellow Christian. Just caring about you—got it?"

She laughed. "Sure, Jack....now carry this board in for me and I want to talk to you about fixing that fan in the kitchen."

"Now that's my friend Dollie talking!" he laughed. "By the way, get back in the car. We have been summoned to the church for a board meeting."

Dollie rolled her eyes as she said, "A what? Now? Tonight?"

"You won't be disappointed. The church got a good contribution to replace the heating/cooling system and it has to be approved by the board before work can begin to install it."

"New heating/cooling system!!!! Wow! That's incredible," she shouted as she threw things in the back seat to make room for Rev. Temple to get in the car.

Rev. Temple and Dollie arrived at the church building about the same time as the rest of the board members. Dollie was secretary of the board and would be needed to prepare the letters and to keep the minutes for the meeting. The group didn't waste any time as they gathered in the dining room around a table and prepared to approve items rapidly.

"Rev. Temple, would you like to start with the main reason for this meeting?" asked the president of the board.

"I certainly will begin. Lewis Walters, president of the local bank, has offered to pay for a new heating/cooling system. He said after watching the community pour into the church yard today with donations and volunteer labor he felt compelled to provide something as well. He had visited the congregation for a service last fall and found the congregation didn't have air conditioning on that record hot night. He said the choir festival will certainly need air conditioning or heating depending on the weather and he had just got a windfall on an investment. He was happy to offer this gift to us if we guarantee that it will be installed in time for the competition in a few weeks."

"Is there any discussion on the matter?"

"I make a motion we accept his offer"

"I make a second to that motion."

"Discussion on the matter?"

"I call for a vote."

"All those in favor, say 'aye" — and those not in favor say 'nay" — and the vote carries."

"Wait, I can't keep up," said Dollie. "Give me a minute to get all this written down."

"The festival is turning out to be a real boost to the congregation. Gifts alone have enabled us to regroup after that horrible expense last year when the hailstorm destroyed the roof and we had water damage."

"The next order of business—."

"Mr. President, I move that all issues to be considered tonight be approved as it appears from the sound of things outside we need to be home in the basement."

"I second that, Mr. President. We trust you in your judgment to hire the proper people and we already have discussed at the coffee shop most of the issues."

"Well, is there any objections?"

"No, call for a vote on the total package."

"All in favor say 'aye' — all opposed say 'nay' — and the motion carries. Is there a motion to adjourn?"

"Oh yes," they all said as they got up from their chairs and headed to the parking lot.

"Wait," called Dollie. "Who made the motion? Ah, what was the motion? Say, what items were approved?"

She looked around and saw no one left except Rev. Temple. She felt like she had just gone thru an inside the building tornado the way they whipped thru the meeting. A big crash of thunder sounded outside as she put her pen away and folded her stenographer pad.

"Jack?" she said as she looked at him puzzled.

"Don't' worry. I'll fill you in on everything, but you'll be very happy at all the things they approved tonight," he replied with a wink. "You and the entire choir will be surprised. Now let's get home. It does look bad out there."

As Dollie crawled into bed her mind continued to think of things that would need to be done. She decided that she would return to the church building and go into the loft and just sit there and meditate a few minutes the next morning. She had done it several times when she was a substitute Sunday school teacher. She found that looking over the empty, quiet building was inspiring. It was there that she would pray for guidance and she would feel the power of the Spirit.

Dollie had substituted for Mack Warner's young adult Bible class when he had a heart attack. The task had been challenging, but she had enjoyed teaching the young adults. The group was always full of fresh new ideas or interpretations and a multitude of questions. That age group had kept her on her toes and many Sunday afternoons she would be searching the Scriptures and Bible commentaries for answers to questions the students had asked.

She had found something special about sitting alone in the silence of the building. The Scripture came to mind as she clicked the light off beside her bed, "Be still and know that I am God." She remembered how peaceful it had been in the church sanctuary and how she felt God's presence. Dollie had found that in the silence she had found the greatness and goodness of God. She felt closer to her creator. Some say they feel his presence on a pond bank while fishing. Others say climbing a mountain brings them closer to God. For her it was simply sitting in the church sanctuary enjoying the quiet.

The silence in her mind was suddenly broken as a memory of the strange sound that she had heard at the church building took over. She remembered how it sounded like a chain and how it seemed to come from a different room. She wondered if it could be something underneath the building like a cat or dog. Then she wondered if she would hear it when she would be sitting in the sanctuary meditating the next day. She rolled over, turned the light on, started to get up but then shrugged her shoulders. "Good night, God. Tomorrow is another day."

She crawled back under the covers and turned out the light. "God, it is good to know you are with me. Thank you and please watch over me as I sleep tonight."

CHAPTER SEVEN

J oan Stacy called a Friday night rehearsal and despite the busy lives of the members the singers promised to be present "on time." Joan had made it clear in her phone call to each member that the choir would need to concentrate and work hard if they were going to be prepared for the festival.

On the agenda for the rehearsal was a new piece. Joan felt it would be the perfect theme song. She wanted to use it for the services the following Sunday to promote the festival. She said it would "be a challenge to learn for Sunday, but she believed they could do it."

As Dollie arrived she saw several vehicles of the choir members in the parking lot when she drove in. She also noticed a couple of unfamiliar cars; a truck with "Bill Owen's Electrical" on the side; and another truck from the local air conditioning dealer. Waving at Dollie was Virgie Meadows as she drove out the exit to the parking lot and Lois Calder as she crossed the street at the crosswalk headed to her house a block away.

The church building had been the center of activities all day with people coming and going. Included in the number was Dollie who had been at the church building three times participating in various committees. With each meeting, her excitement grew as plans were finalized for the "big event."

Joan's negative actions at the Wednesday night choir rehearsal meant something to Dollie now as she fully understood how much pressure would have been on Joan had the group not appointed her festival chairman. The festival planning had taken over her entire life. She had to decline business opportunities for her catering business as there was no time for it.

Still, despite the stress and worry, Dollie found the challenge fulfilling. She thought to herself that Howard would be proud of her leadership abilities. She also thought he would be proud of the congregation which was working together to make a festival that would be special for the entire community.

Thank you, Lord, for your guidance. Thank you for the many volunteers working to make this a wonderful event. Thank you for providing the resources to do the needed preparation for the festival. You are loved—
' *we praise you.*

"The decoration committee must have been working this afternoon," Dollie guessed as she watched committee members Virgie and Lois disappear from sight. "They probably put their materials in the kitchen closet or the multipurpose room. Think I'll take a peak at what they accomplished today."

"Dollie?" Margaret yelled from the church door. "Hurry up! Something strange is in the building?"

Dollie crawled out of her Plymouth and quickly made her way toward the kitchen door. Margaret's comments reminded her of the sound she had heard the day before and again that night. Just thinking about it made her have a cold chill.

"What do you think it is?" questioned Dollie.

Dollie and Margaret had met in the afternoon at Porter's Place for a cup of tea and a cookie. Dollie had expressed her feelings about the strange sound. Unfortunately Margaret saw this as a chance to play a practical joke on Dollie. She had called everyone in the choir and set them up to fool Dollie.

"I don't have a clue—what could it be?" said Margaret as she tried to describe the sound while trying to keep from laughing. "It just sounded one short noise. It was like a chain being dragged."

"Chain being dragged? Oh, come on," responded Dollie while rolling her eyes.

"I heard it too," added Josh poking his head from behind the door.

"Josh!" exclaimed Dollie, surprised to see her good friend. "You're here to sing tonight?"

"Not quite," Josh laughed, "I just stopped by with more of your furniture."

"More of my furniture? What? Uncle John didn't——. Ok, very funny," said a gasping Dollie worried about what her uncle might give away next.

"It's your bed," laughed Josh.

"Just you try to get a homemade cookie again, Mr. McDaniel," laughed Dollie as she tried to be stern.

"Just joking, Dollie. You know that. Now what is this about a ghost?" as the sound of Josh's voice became more like a newspaper reporter.

Sensing this Dollie immediately said in a hurried voice, "Nothing, don't you let Margaret get you all excited about a possible story. There is nothing here for your newspaper. We want the community to be excited about coming to praise God—not coming to see the mysterious spooky church."

"So, you say the church is filled with spirits?" Josh continued.

71

"I didn't say that," said Dollie firmly. "The only spirit here is the Holy Spirit, the spirit of God. Now drop this silly talk about ghosts."

"Margaret, can you describe the sound? Tell me about the strange noise," continued an interested Josh while ducking a playful punch from Dollie. A slightly more serious look came on his face as he continued. "I heard the sound when I came in the door a while ago. It didn't sound like anything I could identify. Maybe we should move the festival. We can't have people's lives at risk with this mysterious being wandering thru the church building."

"Come on, Josh. Do you hear anything now?" responded Dollie in order to prevent Margaret from continuing the story.

Margaret attempted to interrupt, but Dollie raised her voice and continued. "I don't hear anything now. Does anyone hear anything? I don't think so. That's the end of the discussion."

Margaret could hardly contain herself. She was determined to keep from laughing and promptly dived behind the kitchen door. The two had Dollie going this time and Josh was doing a great job in keeping the joke alive.

"Uncle John should be here now," whispered Margaret to Josh as she went by moving toward the multipurpose door. "He would get a kick out of this."

"There are more important things we need to be doing," continued Dollie. "We are here for choir practice. Has anyone seen Joan? She usually arrives first for rehearsals. I don't see her in the choir loft."

"Let's see, the noise was first heard in the multi-purpose room—right? Dollie?" questioned Margaret as she headed back toward the kitchen door. "When you heard it last night where were you standing? At least twice you asked me if I heard it last night. Where were you standing? Ah, I think you were about half way to the kitchen door. It was right about here. Correct?"

Josh took out his trusty notepad and began taking notes. Dollie seeing him began to get uneasy. The last thing the church needed was a community of gossips hearing talk about ghosts in Nickerson Street Church. The festival would be ruined.

"You say she was halfway to the kitchen door?" asked Josh.

"I didn't hear it the first time," continued Margaret, "but I heard it tonight. It's different—not like anything I have ever heard. Dollie, you describe it for us. After all, you were the first to hear it."

Spotting the minister, Dollie shouted for him to come join them. "Jack? Did you hear anything strange in the building today?"

"Now that you mention it, I was standing over by the baptistery this afternoon and there was this strange sound. It was short and quick. Like a—chain being dragged."

Dollie grimaced at his comments. She had hoped to put an end to the discussion with some reassuring words from the minister. Alas, the speculation about the sounds continued. Dollie could only imagine what the town would be saying tomorrow about the church building. Small towns were notorious at spreading gossip and Sassafras Springs was no exception.

"That's what I said!" Margaret shouted. "It sounded like a chain dragging. No, more like—ah, oh, just a slight movement of a chain."

"And why would we hear the sound of a chain being dragged in the church building?" asked Dollie as she hoped to bring sanity to the situation.

"The chains of sin?" suggested Josh.

"Maybe," agreed Jack. "Maybe God is sending us a message."

"I know you're joking, but you had better be careful what you say with a reporter standing here. You'll open the newspaper next week and see your name in headlines proclaiming that 'Church Spirit Speaks at Nickerson Street Church,'" laughed Dollie as she attempted to make the situation humorous rather than serious.

"You know, that isn't bad. You want to write the article for me?" tormented Josh.

"You two are just a load of laughs tonight. Margaret and I had better get to the choir loft before Joan starts or we will be in trouble. Josh, if you have time you might drop by and play a game of checkers with Uncle John—oh wait, he'll probably donate more furniture for the sale. Forget that idea."

"By the way, where is Joan? Should she be in the choir loft already," asked Margaret. "You don't suppose the spirit got her? Oh my, what if this spirit kidnaps people?"

"Margaret," began Dollie, "Are you nuts? Now quit all of this talk. Where is Joan?"

Voices could be heard in the kitchen and Josh had disappeared. Dollie hoped he had gone to Uncle John's to play checkers which would keep him away from writing an article about ghosts in the church. She turned to Margaret and asked her to go on to the choir loft and tell Joan that she would be there soon but that she wanted to see what committee was working in the kitchen.

"Well, I want to know what is going on in the kitchen too," said Margaret as she followed Dollie.

As Dollie opened the door to the kitchen the entire choir who were hiding there started making spooky sounds to see if they could scare Dollie. She jerked away from the door and looked toward Margaret with panic in her eyes. Margaret burst out laughing and Josh quickly opened the door and pulled Dollie inside the kitchen where everyone was laughing.

"That was mean, people," shook Dollie as she tried to regroup.

"We're sorry Dollie," laughed Margaret. "I couldn't help myself. It was just too good a trick to pull. Please forgive me."

Dollie rolled her eyes and looked at the whole group. "What can I say? You were all in on this? Wow. I feel honored — I guess."

Finally, after the group stopped laughing and things were quieted down, Dollie turned to Joan and said, "Let's get everyone to the loft. This crazy talk about a spirit or some such thing has got to stop," a determined Dollie said as she left the kitchen on her way to the loft. "Come on, everyone. Let's get to the choir loft. There isn't anything going to get you tonight."

"She seems rather determined," began Joan. "Let's get to rehearsing."

The group all cheered and headed toward the doorway to the sanctuary on their way to the choir loft. Laughing and joking continued as the group celebrated the trick they had played on their good friend Dollie.

CHAPTER EIGHT

As the choir members were walking across the sanctuary floor to the stairs the lights flickered a couple of times and then darkness swallowed the group. The usually pleasant room was suddenly strange and a little frightening as the group groped their way to the stairs. Sounds of nervous laughs could be heard along with comments about the "spirits will get you."

The choir members had been in the sanctuary thousands of times, but now every item in the room seemed to be in a new location. The distance to the stairs felt much farther. The sound of different people groaning or saying "Ouch" continued as they bumped their way across the room.

"Who is leading this group?" questioned John Paterno, the newest member of the choir. "If we end up back in the kitchen you can assume we are going in circles."

"Very funny," laughed the group.

A crash like the sound of thunder was heard just as the front door of the sanctuary flew open. A bang sounded as the door hit the wall. A cool breeze rushed across the room brushing against each of the choir members.

"Eeek!" screamed several of the women.

"I feel like spider webs are all over me," said Jessica Blanden.

"It's just a breeze," answered Dollie.

"Did anyone hear the weather report?" asked Lincoln Madison. "I thought it was to be clear all weekend."

"You think we should check for tornadoes?" asked Steve Elsea as he remembered the tornado that struck the church during one rehearsal, "or do tornadoes not strike twice in the same place?"

"I'll get the door," said Lincoln.

Lincoln Madison felt his way to the door and as he started to shut it noticed the lights in the houses across the street. He stepped out into the foyer of the church building and could see the lights still shining in every direction.

"We are the only ones without lights," Lincoln shouted back to the group. "You can see the street lights in all directions. The houses across the street all have lights. Do you suppose lightening struck our building?"

The choir reached the top steps of the stairs and felt their way to their usual seats in the choir loft. Despite the darkness the members were determined to begin rehearsing as soon as the lights came back on.

"Do you think anyone else is in the building?" questioned Steve Elsea. "Someone should be finding out what caused the lights to go out. It could be that a breaker switch in the breaker box needs to be switched back on. If no one else is here we may sit in darkness for a long time. Maybe one of us should check the box. Does anyone know where it is?"

"Steve, I'll go with you," volunteered Lincoln. "It should be in the kitchen or the storage room."

The two men felt their way along the wall and started down the stairs. Meanwhile Joan started explaining her plans for the musical portion of the festival. She listed various musical compositions the group would need to learn and when each performance would occur.

"And so you see," continued Joan, "we do have a lot to do before the festival in three weeks."

"I don't think I rolled my windows up on the car," panicked Mary Lynn Sumner, "and it sounded like it would be pouring down rain in a few minutes."

"Hurry Mary Lynn," responded Joan. "We have a lot of work to do."

"Here's a flashlight I always carry in my purse," offered Colleen Marx knowing it would be hard for Mary Lynn to find her way down the stairs and out to the parking lot.

"Thanks for the flashlight," she replied. "I'll be back as quickly as I can."

"Why didn't you offer the flashlight to Steve and Lincoln?" asked Dollie.

"Men walk around in the dark all the time," she laughed. "Actually I didn't think of it until they were gone. Shouldn't they be back by now?"

Dollie thought about the two men who had gone to rescue the choir from darkness and Mary Lynn who was out to save her car from damage from the rain. She paused to ask God to protect her friends.

Lord, be with Steve and Lincoln. Help them to find the problem with the lights. Protect Mary Lynn as she goes to her car. Bring all of them back quickly and allow the choir to have their much needed rehearsal. We are here to prepare for the festival. We seek to praise your name in song. Amen.

Mary Lynn's steps could be heard by the choir members as she went down the squeaky stairs and across the sanctuary floor. Just as Mary Lynn shut the door the lights came back on. Joan wasted no time. She quickly started the vocal warm up drills and had Sherrie Bennett begin distributing music folders that had been prepared the night before. Things were back on schedule.

"Ooo-ahh-eee-aye," vocalized the choir. "Noo-nah-nee-nay, moo-mah-mee-may, foo-fah-fee-fay, goo-gah-gee gay."

Joan's professional training had led her to use warm up drills. Unfortunately, the choir thought the warm up drills were stupid at first and there were some unpleasant moments, but the drills quickly began to make a difference in the sound of the choir. With the improvement of quality in singing came the acceptance and insistence by the choir for the drills.

Joan used different silly syllables and a variety of rhythms to make them unique and interesting. She also taped accompaniments that jazzed up the sound of the drills. This made the drills fun and interesting for the choir. The drills also helped to bring everybody to the proper mood for a successful rehearsal.

"Is anyone cold?" asked Robert and Ralph together. The twins often finished each other's sentence if they weren't already saying the same words. They also sensed what the other was thinking. Tonight they had both realized that they were cold. The weather outside had been in the 80's when they arrived and most had dressed for that kind of temperature. Apparently the weather had changed drastically since they had arrived.

"Oooooo! It must be the spirit!" offered Margaret. "They say you feel cold and damp when a spirit is in the room."

"Maggie!" whined Dollie as she felt hurt by Margaret's comment. Dollie had trusted her friend with the information they had talked about at the coffee shop. She couldn't believe that Margaret had organized the entire choir to make fun of her and now was continuing to make fun of her. She would think twice about telling Margaret anything from now on.

"Enough is enough. Yes, I heard a strange sound. Yes, I allowed my imagination to take over—BUT THERE IS NO GHOST OR SPIRIT IN THIS PLACE! Now drop it!."

"Well, sorrrr—eee!" replied Margaret. "Aren't we touchy tonight?"

"Choir," began Joan, "Let's all stand and sing our special song from last Sunday. Sherrie, please play each part's first note."

Steven and Lincoln were heard coming up the stairs. Mary Lynn lost hold of the front door and it slammed against the wall again. Everyone jumped as nerves were beginning to get on edge.

"Sorry," shouted Mary Lynn knowing that she had probably upset Joan. "The wind caught it. I don't remember wind coming in the building like this before. Something is strange tonight."

"Hey, don't you start now too," groaned Dollie.

"That's what I was telling Lincoln," said Steve. "The building usually doesn't have a breeze in it and wind is blowing everywhere. Do you feel it?"

"Yes, you're right Lincoln," chimed in Ralph and Robert.

"Where is it coming from?" asked Margaret Cushing. "It's almost like the wind is coming from under the floor."

"People! Let's keep our minds on practicing," interrupted Joan.

"Margaret is right. It's coming from the floor," agreed Colleen. "What would cause that?"

"I don't have any idea," replied Margaret.

The lights flickered and the choir found themselves in total darkness again. A tapping began. It sounded like it was coming from the area of the pulpit.

"What the—?" muttered Steve. "Look!"

The choir members stood in amazement. A small bright column of light was coming from the ceiling to the pulpit. There was no other light in the sanctuary. For the moment there was not a sound to be heard. No breeze was felt.

"Cling-ching!"

"There it is again!" shouted Dollie. She covered her mouth quickly as she knew she had turned everyone's attention back to the persisting unique sound that kept invading the church building. "What was that sound? What was causing it? Now what was this light that glowed in the sanctuary? Was it a sign from God?" she asked herself.

As the choir continued to lean forward in the loft taking in the entire view, another burst of wind came blowing thru the auditorium. The curtains at the back of the podium suddenly lifted off the floor and waved in the breeze just as the light came back on.

"God, Almighty! What is going on?" yelled Lincoln.

"There has to be a reasonable explanation," said Dollie while shivering inside with no possible idea of what could be causing these strange events.

The lights flashed on and off again. The column of light disappeared, but a whining noise could be heard. Again, it seemed to be coming from underneath the floor. Joan encouraged the choir to take their seats again. She offered encouragement remembering a song from "The King and I" where the little boy was encouraged to whistle when he was scared.

"Sherrie, I think there were some candles in the organ bench left from the Christmas program," said Joan. "Would you please pass them out to the choir and let's try to get our minds back on the rehearsal. We all know that our minds are running wild after all that talk about spirits earlier. We know that can't be what is happening."

Sherrie found the candles and passed them out to the choir members. One by one the candles were lit and as light began to fill the corners of darkness in the sanctuary the choir members began to return to reality. With a determined effort, the choir returned to singing. Soon the lights returned and the candles were extinguished. Music filled the sanctuary with joy and praise to God.

"Well, that wraps up the rehearsal tonight," said Joan with joy in her tone. "You all did a remarkably good job tonight, especially when you consider all of the interruptions."

"You know, there wasn't a cloud in the sky when I went out to roll my windows up on the car," said Mary Lynn.

"The breaker box was fine too," began Steve, "We didn't fix the lights. They just seemed to come on by themselves."

"That's right," supported Lincoln. "No explanation for it."

"Well, what about the column of light we saw?" asked Margaret.

"What about the tapping? Sound of a pulled chain? The wind coming and going throughout the building with no explanation?" they all asked each other.

"Everything is alright now," reassured Dollie as the choir members began to gather their things to leave.

"NO-ooooo!" Joan screamed as the lights went out again. Just as quickly a bright light was shining thru the stained glass window at the back of the choir loft. Few had ever really noticed the window as the light from the sun was on the other side of the building. Few realized it was a stained glass window. Its darkness made it look like an old painting in need of cleaning.

The choir turned toward the now brightly lit stained glass window behind the choir loft. It was spectacular. The stained glass formed a picture of the Good Shepherd feeding his sheep. The choir stood in silence admiring the beauty of the picture. It was almost speaking to them.

"Joan, are you alright," asked Dollie when she spotted her on the floor."

"No," she sighed. "It can't be. It can't be his ghost."

In unison the entire choir turned and stared at Joan with mouths forming the word "Ghosts?"

"What are you talking about, Joan?" asked Margaret.

"Whose ghost?" a stunned Colleen asked.

"My husband, Sidney Smith's," continued Joan. "He donated the window. See his name at the bottom?"

The choir in unison mouthed the word in unison, "Husband?"

"Joan, that's ridiculous," said Margaret as she walked toward the window to see if the name was where she said it was. "You were never married. We all know that—something about your career in New York—oh my gosh! She is right. Sidney Smith. There it is as plain as day in the corner of the window. Who did you say he was?"

Joan quickly gathered her things refusing to say anything more. She raced down the steps and out the door before anyone could catch her.

"Dollie, do you know what she is talking about?" said the choir in unison.

"Not a clue. I never knew she was married. Not a clue."

CHAPTER NINE

"Uncle John," called Dollie as she entered his house. "Are you up? I have some questions to ask you. Are you awake?"

"Where have you been?" a worried Uncle John said. "I thought you said you were coming right over after choir practice to share some ice cream I bought today. I was hoping to have a good visit with you. Didn't you say you would be over about nine p.m.? It's after eleven now."

There stood Uncle John dressed in blue pajamas with a print of half moons all over them. On top of his head was his New York Yankees hat that Howard had bought when the two of them went to New York a few years earlier. John always had a smile on his face and a little moustache that seemed to twitter when he told a joke. He was always full of fun and was a joy to be around.

"Where have I been, you ask?" said Dollie as she removed the hat from Uncle John's head. "Where are you going?"

Dollie patted his cheek with the hat and gave him a wink. She knew he cared for her safety and she appreciated it. He had filled a deep loneliness in her life after her husband died. Uncle John had always had a joke to tell when she appeared lonely or depressed. His numerous riddles and stories could brighten anyone's day.

"So that's where I put it," he laughed putting the cap on the table near by. "So tell me, what happened tonight. I can tell it must be big."

Dollie gave him a hug and nodded like she was getting ready to tell him. He pulled her over to a comfortable chair and patted the seat motioning for her to sit. Uncle John began watching her closely as he sensed that something was not quite right. In a short time she got up and went to the kitchen. Uncle John quickly followed her and got the ice cream out of the freezer while Dollie got a pan, some milk and hot chocolate mix.

Dollie remained quiet. She leaned on the counter and began shuffling the cookbooks that were on a bookcase part of the built-ins.

"Do you think you'll like Rocky Road or Butter Pecan ice cream?" he asked.

"I'm not very hungry," she replied.

"You start talking then because you can't leave until you let me in on the story that is flooding your mind. I can tell you are overloaded with thoughts. Better share. You know you will feel better if you talk it out."

Dollie turned the stove on and poured some milk in the pan.

"Well," she said.

"Well?" an eager Uncle John moved forward to hear her.

"I've got to keep Josh from putting an article in the newspaper," she mumbled in a worried voice. "It will kill the choir festival if he prints it."

Dollie reached over and stirred the milk, poured the hot chocolate in the pan and stirred it some more. She took the top off the cookie jar and found nothing in it so replaced the lid. Tapping her foot nervously, she looked at Uncle John like she needed to talk.

"What can I do, Uncle John?" she continued.

"My dear little Dollie, I can't help you if you don't tell me what happened," he said as he continued to press her to tell him about the events of the night. "You say there were several things that happened? Just start from the beginning. You can tell me anything."

Dollie remained quiet as she shuffled the cookbooks on the shelf again. She opened the refrigerator door and shut it; opened a couple of drawers and closed them back; and finally sat down at the kitchen table with a gasp.

Uncle John followed her every movement throughout the kitchen. His gaze followed her back and forth to the refrigerator where she kept opening the door and to the pantry where she had played as a small girl years earlier. Now he stared at her as she sat at the kitchen table looking helpless. Dollie's behavior was worrying him.

"So, Dollie," began Uncle John again. "What happened?"

"Hm-m-m?" she thought. "How do I tell all of this? I don't understand anything that happened tonight."

"So how does Josh enter the picture? I thought you were at the church for choir practice?" Uncle John questioned.

Dollie crossed her legs and then pulled one leg up under her and sat on it like she did when a small girl. She put her head down on the table feeling the helplessness of the moment.

"By the way, Margaret called and was looking for you," continued Uncle John as he interrupted her thoughts.

"Maggie?" repeated Dollie in an alarmed tone as she reflected on what had occurred at the choir rehearsal. "We did have some unusual things happen tonight and knowing Maggie—she is probably calling everyone in town to tell them about it. I wish she wasn't such a gossip."

"I see," supported Uncle John. "Care to share the true story?"

Dollie could only think about how Magaret had tormented her and embarrassed her. She knew she shouldn't be angry about it. Margaret didn't do it to hurt her, but it did. Then suddenly Dollie realized that if Margaret talked to Josh the entire night's events could be in the newspaper the next day.

Oh, Lord, please keep Margaret from—ah, Lord, help Margaret to remain calm about the things that happened tonight.

"What in the world happened, my pretty niece?" asked an intrigued Uncle John.

"Well, I'm not sure how to describe everything or where to begin. Or what was real and what was not. I'm so confused right now."

"You have had some night," replied Uncle John. "I've never seen you like this."

"I've never been like this."

There was a lengthy period of silence. Uncle John wanted to know what had happened, but he knew there were times when a person needs to be quiet and by doing so demonstrate more support for an individual. Uncle John looked at the refrigerator and then at the stove. He decided it would be more affective if he let Dollie decide when to tell him the story. He was confident she would before she left. He got a couple of bowls to put ice cream in and then a couple of spoons.

Dollie got up from the kitchen table and went in the living room again; kicked off her shoes; turned the television on with the remote control; and thought about the events of the evening as she sat on the soft divan and tried to relax. Uncle John quietly returned the ice cream to the freezer and went in to the living room to join Dollie.

Uncle John looked at the television and then to the newspaper he had picked up to disguise his desire to hear what Dollie had to say. He tried his best to look unconcerned. Suddenly he realized he was alone in the room. He looked both ways and stretched to see if Dollie had gone back in the kitchen. No Dollie was to be found. He looked outside on the front porch. Dollie sometimes liked to swing on the two seater swing at the end of the front porch when she had something on her mind. As he looked outside he spotted a long black car parked across the street.

"Hmmmm? Wonder who that is?" questioned Uncle John. "Never mind now, Dollie. Hey, Dollie!! Where did you go? Hey! Dollie, are you here?"

Uncle John toured the rooms of the house. He checked the basement and found it in total darkness. He checked the attic and found it equally dark. There was no Dollie.

"Dollie!!" shouted Uncle John in a strong voice. "Dollie, are you alright? Where are you?"

Uncle John went out the back door and walked around the outside of the house. He noticed the black car was gone when he reached the front porch, but was distracted from thinking about the car when he felt a gentle nudge at his ankle. Looking down he saw Charlie, the neighbor cat that would take walks with Dollie.

"She must not be too far off if Charlie is here. Charlie would have chased after her. Now where can that niece be?"

The cat meowed and continued to rub Uncle John's ankles. Not wanting to kick the cat away, he edged his way to the porch swing and sat down. He again looked every direction for Dollie and called her name. There was no Dollie to be seen or heard. He ran his hand down Charlie's neck and body resulting in a purr of satisfaction from the cat.

"I mentioned Marge," thought Uncle John as he did a replay of their conversation when Dollie got there. "Ah, maybe she has gone to see Marge. That has to be it, but why didn't she tell me. Why is her car still here? Why did she leave without a word? Something strange is going on. I'm going to have to do some investigating. We can't have Dollie getting wrapped up in some mystery. Right, Charlie?"

He looked at the cat that had climbed into his lap. "So, Charlie," he questioned, "Have you seen Dollie?"

Uncle John continued to pat the cat and rocked the swing back and forth as he thought how he was going to get to the bottom of the situation. Of course he did not know what had happened at the choir practice. He had to admit to himself that he was lost until he knew what had happened. So where had Dollie disappeared and what was she doing?

The silence was suddenly broken with the sound of a siren and flashing red lights. Officer Brown rolled into the driveway with his patrol car. Jumping out he yelled to Uncle John to get the hose.

"For the love of God!" shouted Uncle John, startled by the intrusion into his thoughts. "What did you do that for? Going to arrest me? Oh wait! It isn't Dollie? She is alright?"

"There's smoke coming from your kitchen!" hollered Officer Brown.

"What??" shouted an excited Uncle John, "Oh my, Lord! the hot chocolate! Dollie must have left it on the stove."

"You stay here, Uncle John," directed Officer Brown. "I'll go in the back door with my fire extinguisher."

"I'll get the water hose!" Uncle John shouted back.

The sound of an approaching fire truck could be heard with sirens going full blast and getting louder by the minute. Another patrol car pulled up with lights flashing and two policemen jumped out and started directing traffic as people came to see what was happening.

Uncle John was shaking and pacing the back yard. "Dollie, where are you!"

In a short time, Officer Brown came out of the back door with a smoking scorched pan of hot chocolate. He placed it on the ground and took the hose from Uncle John. Hissing sounds could be heard as the cold water hit the extremely hot pan.

Standing there in silence for a few seconds, the two men watched the pot run over with water. Officer Brown assured Uncle John he could turn off the water as the fire was out. The fire truck was then sent on its way and the other police car left. Officer Brown and Uncle John stood there staring at the pan.

"We could have lost the house," worried Uncle John. "Dollie, where are you?"

"I'm right here," replied Dollie as she came around the corner of the house breathing deeply. She noticed the two with the water hose. "Hey, are you planting flowers this time of night? Or burying a corpse in the backyard?"

Raising his eyebrow, Uncle John pulled Dollie close to him and hugged her. Seeing the pan, Dollie suddenly gasped. She pushed Uncle John back and looked at him with tears in her eyes.

"Yes, you nearly burned the house down," replied Uncle John in a weak voice still shaking from the near tragedy.

"What are you talking — oh, the hot chocolate — oh my!" said Dollie as she became weak in the knees.

Dollie rushed inside the house and grimaced at the smell of burnt milk and chocolate. She looked at the ceiling now displaying a black design directly over the stove where the pan had been. The ceiling was marked with soot. Dollie was not pleased at the results of her carelessness, yet she was thankful there was not more damage done. She didn't need extra work, but it was obvious that she would need to come to Uncle John's to help clean up this mess. As she walked from room to room she could see it was going to be more than just the kitchen that would need to be cleaned.

"Tonight has been too stressful for me. I need to rest. Uncle John, you are going home with me and will stay in the guest room until we get this mess cleaned up. I am so sorry. You know I didn't mean to do this."

"Sit down and start talking," demanded Uncle John. "I can't help you unless you talk to me. This stress you have shown tonight has got to be brought under control. I can't handle it. You're not acting like yourself. Now what happened tonight and what is wrong?"

"Officer Brown, have you got time to go to the Nickerson Street Church?" Dollie asked.

"Sure, I was just making a few rounds to insure everything is quiet," replied Officer Brown. "What's the problem?"

"I'm not sure," she begins, "but something is strange at the church. I think someone is trying to sabotage the choir festival."

Both Officer Brown and Uncle John dropped their mouths open at this revelation announced by Dollie.

"Dollie, you can't be serious!" said a startled Uncle John. "Who would do something like that?"

"I don't know, but tonight there were a lot of things that happened that didn't have any reasonable explanation. Officer Brown, are you ready to go?" continued Dollie.

"Let me call the station first to let them know where I am going," Officer Brown replied.

"Well, let me get changed. I'm going too," said Uncle John.

"No, you get packed and I'll come back for you. No one could sleep in a house smelling like this. Oh, I'm sorry Uncle John." She hugged him tight and kissed his cheek.

"Ok, you two go on and figure out what is happening. I'll be ready when you get back."

CHAPTER TEN

"How are we going to get in the church building?" asked Officer Brown as they approached the church.

"I brought the key," said a nervous Dollie. "I'm church clerk so they gave me a key for such situations, but I see by the tag on this one that it is actually Rev. Temple's. I must have grabbed the wrong one on the key holder at home."

The church stood in total darkness as it usually did at this time of night. As they came closer to the building Dollie remembered how bright the light was in the parking lot when she walked to her car in contrast to the previous night when it had been pitch black. Now the parking lot was totally dark again. She had noticed there was a full moon but the parking lot was totally black. At least there was a logical explanation as she noticed the large shade trees were preventing the light from hitting the parking lot at this time.

Dollie was struck by the beauty of the night. There was a slight breeze blowing thru her hair. The smell of lilacs drifted through the air from the shrubbery fence of bushes separating the church parking lot from the neighbor's yard. She found all of this reassuring. The shrubs were in full bloom a good two months early due to the unseasonable warmth and would be a beautiful sight for those coming to the festival.

"Yes, there was an explanation for everything and she and Officer Brown would find the answers," she thought to herself. "I just need an impartial person to point them out to me."

Dollie placed the key in the lock and opened the door. Stepping inside she looked every direction, but couldn't see a thing because of the darkness. She reached for the light switch. She heard it click, but no lights came on.

"Hm-m-m?" she mumbled feeling her neck and shoulders starting to tighten.

"What are we looking for?" asked a confused Officer Brown. Dollie had remained quiet on the trip to the church building as she didn't particularly want to explain things to Officer Brown. Unfortunately, Officer Brown was now beginning to think that the problem wasn't the church building, but rather Dollie. She was acting completely out of character.

"There were several unusual things that happened during the choir rehearsal tonight. I am hoping that you will be able to help me understand what actually happened rather than what we thought happened."

"Example?" said an even more confused Officer Brown.

Dollie grimaced. She wasn't sure she wanted to share with Officer Brown how the entire choir had been tormenting her earlier about the chain noise. Nor did she want to tell how they all thought ghosts or spirits had invaded the church building. On the other hand, she wanted answers to the mysterious sounds and events of the evening so the church could focus on hosting the church choir festival.

"The lights won't work," remarked Dollie with a shake in her voice.

"Here," replied Officer Brown as he began to take charge. "Let me try."

With a click of the switch the lights quickly lit up the entire room. Dollie looked at him with her eyes as wide as they could get. The reassurance she had felt outside the building had completely disappeared. She tried to turn the switch off to see if the lights would go off for her. They did. She tried to turn the lights off to see if the lights would come on. She shook her head in disbelief as they came on.

Officer Brown, seeing how shaken she was attempted to calm her down and explained that she probably had touched the wrong switch. He pointed to another switch beside the one he had used. Dollie gasped and explained that there was only one switch earlier in the day. She felt goose bumps on her neck and arms. She shivered with fear. Her mind was filling with questions as she began telling Officer Brown about the events of the evening.

She explained how she had heard a strange noise like a chain clinking. She told how the entire choir had seen a light shining from the ceiling to the pulpit. She described the strange whining noise and how the curtains were lifted into the air behind the pulpit.

"Well, you did have some interesting things happening," responded Officer Brown with a raised eyebrow. "So, what do you think happened?"

"That's not all," Dollie continued getting more excited in her commentary concerning the strange events. She glanced toward the choir loft.

"There's more?" mumbled Officer Brown while rolling his eyes and looking away from her to prevent laughing.

Dollie pulled Officer Brown by his shirt sleeve as she led him to the choir loft. Stopping for a second she swallowed hard and shook her whole body as to shake away the fear she felt.

"Are you alright?" asked Officer Brown in a concerned tone.

"Yes, I know it seems like I'm crazy," she began, "but these things really happened."

Dollie paused again as she looked up the stairs to the choir loft. She remembered how a sudden light beamed down on the choir members as they were standing in total darkness. Step by step she climbed the squeaking stairs. Each sound made the room seem even more scary. Slowly, Dollie positioned Officer Brown and herself in front of the stained glass window.

"So?" waited Officer Brown. "What happened?"

"Herb, we were standing in the dark wondering what we should do and what was going to happen next. No, that's not right. Some of us were wondering what was going on, but others had decided to leave. Any way, we were all making our way to the stairs when it happened!"

"And—?" pressed Officer Brown as he attempted to make sense of this story.

"We were standing in complete darkness and then this sudden light blasted us. We were blinded at first," continued Dollie.

Officer Brown looked at her and wondered if he should contact her son in Chicago. He thought to himself how pitiful it was to see this wonderful person breaking up like this mentally. He would definitely talk to Uncle John when they returned to his place.

"We were standing right here in the choir loft and this light suddenly was shining through the stained glass window. I don't think I had really looked at the window before because it looked so dirty. No light was able to shine through it. It really had never been attractive. Some of the choir members thought it was a painting. They were stunned when they saw it was a beautiful stained glass window. And I do mean beautiful. It was breath taking—and amazingly none of us had ever seen it lit up before. And no one had any idea where the light was coming from."

Officer Brown continued to look at Dollie with a curious feeling that at some point a movie camera would appear and he would be on television as the subject of some joke. He looked at her eyes for a sign that she was joking, but only found eyes that were stressed and serious. Without a doubt in his mind, Officer Brown believed that Dollie believed everything she had said.

"Dollie," he began, "I will need to contact the station to let them know where I am."

"You called them on the way over," Dollie snapped knowing that Officer Brown didn't believe her. "You don't understand how frightening this is. We host the Choir Festival in three weeks. We can't have strange things like this happening. The people will never come to our congregation again. We have to find what is going on."

"Do you think there are ghosts here?" asked a worried Officer Brown.

"I don't know what it is," said a frustrated Dollie.

"Let me call a couple of people," said Officer Brown as he made plans to check her story with other choir members. "I'll get back with you tomorrow after I have a chance to check some things."

"You mean, 'check me out,'" snapped Dollie again.

"Dollie Mae Burgess!" said a surprised Officer Brown. "We have been friends for many years. Howard, your husband, was my coach in the Little League and your son and I were in the same 4-H Club.. Remember? You know I think the world of you. It's my job to check things out. You be patient with me. I'll get back with you tomorrow after I have had time to investigate."

"Now don't forget we are having a big garage sale here tomorrow. Come to think of it, I better get Uncle John moved to my house and get to bed. It will be a busy day. Everyone will be too busy for ghosts to be chasing us around—ha!"

"Cling-chink!"

"That's a better attitude Dollie," cheered Officer Brown. "Ah, did you hear that? What was that?"

He turned toward Dollie who was pale as a ghost.

"You heard it?" said Dollie.

"Yes," he replied.

"That's the noise I have been hearing. We can't find what it is. Do you have any idea? Which direction did it come from? I'm totally confused and it sounds when you least expect it. No warning—just a strange noise."

"That's the noise? Seems harmless enough, but it is strange. Humm?"

"Look Herb, you have been a good friend for years. I remember you as one of my best students in Sunday school. I know you care and you do your best in every way. I don't believe there are ghosts here but there were so many strange things that don't seem to have an explanation. I need to have answers before Josh gets a hold of the story and prints it in the newspaper."

"Dollie, you know Josh wouldn't print something that would hurt our town, the churches or you," he stressed.

"Perhaps you are right. I'm just a little sensitive right now due to the festival. I want it to be a big success and maybe the pressure of that has me not thinking straight. On the other hand, it was the entire choir here and we all saw these things. How can I be expected to ignore that?"

"Good point," Officer Brown responded. "I'll get right on it Dollie. There is an answer."

"I hope so and I hope we figure it out first before it starts spreading all over town in gossip," replied Dollie. "Let's lock up and get to Uncle John's. Thanks for coming by Herb."

CHAPTER ELEVEN

The next morning Dollie was awakened to the sounds of the neighbor cat meowing outside her window. There was no time to jog around the block today. She quickly jumped in the shower, ate breakfast and dressed. By 6 a.m. she arrived at the big sale at the church building. Already Margaret was there directing customers around the building.

Ralph and Robert were busy selling baked goods donated by a variety of friends of the choir. There were cinnamon rolls, donuts, and hot coffee which were selling well on this surprisingly cool morning. Other items available included twenty loaves of bread including two raisin; twenty three pies (eleven different varieties); nineteen cakes and an assortment of other baked treats. Dollie looked them over and realized she had failed to make some for the sale.

Ike Winston had sent twelve dozen cookies. No doubt they would disappear in a hurry once it was known that Ike had made the treats. Mrs. Culley had sent eight boxes of her homemade fudge. She was well known for her delicious candies and every year was a favorite to win a large number of blue ribbons at the local fair. There was also a collection of jams and jellies sent by Grace Markham, the owner of the local bed and breakfast.

Remembering she wanted to buy a few things, Dollie stopped by the display of Julia Ferguson's knitting and selected an afghan. Then she moved to Lincoln Madison's display items and took a closer look at the recliners that he had brought. She knew that Rev. Temple would enjoy having one of those. She toured the multi-purpose room quickly knowing that she would not have much time to do shopping for herself and then paid for the lovely green and blue afghan and chair. She took the afghan to her car where she had stored a "sold" sign to put on one of the chairs. She would have to remember to ask Josh if he would take the chair to her house.

When she re-entered the building she stopped by "her" table that Uncle John had donated thanks to Josh's helpfulness in delivering it to the sale. She remembered how she had intended to place it in the living room in front of the windows. She had planned to place some of Uncle John's tulips in a vase that her mother had given her when a small girl. She nodded approvingly at the vision of the tulips on that table.

"Well, this is a good cause and there is enough furniture in the living room already," she thought. "It would have made an inviting sight to enter the house and see the table and bouquet. Well, it is better here than in Uncle John's attic."

"Dollie," yelled Margaret. "I need some help over here. Can you help me for a couple of minutes?"

Dollie looked in the direction of Margaret and saw seven people in line to pay for items from the sale. She quickly went to Margaret's rescue and began totaling purchases and accepting money. She was amazed at the variety of things the people were buying from the sale. There were several items that she had not seen. She was going to have to make a more thorough examination of the multi-purpose room before everything was gone.

When she saw that Margaret had everything under control again, Dollie slipped away to the kitchen to see the twins and find out if they needed help. Again, they were doing an outstanding job. They had enlisted several choir members and set up a work schedule. Dollie had to admit that she would not have done a better job. Everything seemed to be going like clockwork.

As she was walking back toward the multi-purpose room there was a familiar sound.

"Cling-chink!"

"Did you hear it?" she yelled while looking around at everyone.

The people stopped and looked at her with startled expressions. The calm, collected, always in control Dollie was looking panicked. Margaret quickly rushed to her side.

"Dollie," began Margaret, "you will have everyone storming out of the building."

"No, I think they will be calling Uncle John to come get me. I'm sorry, but I heard that noise again."

"What noise?" asked Annie Reynolds.

"I heard something strange," added Jolee Barnes. "It was like a chain moving."

"I heard it too. What was it?" asked Harrison Caldwell. "I didn't think it was like a chain. It was more—ah, I don't know. It was strange."

"Now you have done it!" Margaret whispered as she took Dollie away from the group.

"Maggie, thanks for bringing me back to my senses," said Dollie. "I was relaxed and the sound sent me back to last night. Officer Brown and I came back last night—well, we didn't find anything, but he heard the sound too."

"I'm sorry we all tormented you with the joke last night. We all felt pretty bad once we got involved with all the strange things that happened later on. We should have known better. It got all of us thinking wild things too. It just grew."

"Exactly!" said Dollie in a stronger voice. "You are right. Where was our faith in God last night? There was no reason for us to carry on with fear like that. 'If God before us, who can be against us,' says the Scripture."

"Morning Margaret and Dollie," began Rev. Temple. "Sale looks like it is going great."

Dollie coughed to cover their conversation and turned with a smile on her face to greet the preacher. Margaret waved to him and rushed back to her post at the cash table.

"I was surprised to run into Uncle John this morning. He said he had moved in. What's that about?" asked Rev. Temple.

"Well, I sort of nearly burned his house down last night," Dollie mumbled.

"You didn't? What in the world were you doing?" said Rev. Temple with a shocked expression on his face.

"I'll tell you later. It looks like we have a big crowd on hand. God has certainly blessed us this week."

"That he has," agreed Rev. Temple.

The sale continued but rumors floated around about a strange noise being heard in all of the rooms. By the time Josh arrived at 8:30 a.m. the rumors had grown into "unsubstantiated facts." Josh had his trusty notebook pad and was taking notes and appeared to be interviewing people. Dollie knew this was not a good sign. As soon as she had an opportunity to leave her post she went to talk to Josh.

"Josh," she began, "great to see you here. I figured as hard as you worked bringing furniture for different people that you would sleep-in."

"Very funny," laughed Josh. "I did think about it. I was in bed sleeping soundly when the phone rang from someone telling me Nickerson Street Church was haunted. Are you going to duck the issue of strange noises again? That is all I have been hearing since I got here. I talked to seven people before I even got to the door."

"Oh, no," said Dollie in a calm voice like everything was fine and she was mocking him.

"The cat is out of the bag, Can't hide it. Now what is going on?" Josh asked.

"Do you hear anything?" questioned Dollie as she desperately tried to settle the issue.

"Officer Brown said he did," responded Josh. "He said he was not scared or concerned, but the more he thought about it the more it didn't make sense."

"So he called you?" said Dollie gritting her teeth that Officer Brown would report things happening in town to the editor of the newspaper. "I really need to talk to him."

"So there is something to the story?"

"Well, there you have it. All I can tell you apparently Officer Brown has told you."

"You sure are a stubborn woman, Dollie."

"Just because someone heard a sound doesn't mean there is a story. It certainly doesn't mean the building is haunted," continued Dollie.

"Haunted? Now we are getting somewhere," he said as he opened his notebook and got his pen ready to write.

"Josh McDaniel, if you write something about this I will never talk to you again," she blurted out in the middle of a group. They all turned and looked at her. Dollie turned a bright red with embarrassment. "Sorry, we were having a slight disagreement. It's nothing to worry about."

"That may be," said Josh as he eyed Dollie carefully. "You know, I thought it was a joke, but from your actions I am beginning to think there is something going on. Level with me."

"Josh, do you think I would play a joke on you?"

"No and that's why I know there is more to this story. So what is going on?"

"Keep your voice down," said Dollie. "I don't want people to hear this craziness. They will—ah—isn't that strange?" Her head turned toward the front entrance as she stretched to see who it was.

"What?" said Josh a bit startled at her change in conversation. "A fortune teller? I'm surprised you had a fortune teller come as a fundraiser."

"No, I didn't do that. No, ah? Josh, I'm so confused. Why did they make me festival director. I'm so stressed out this week I can't make smart decisions."

"Nonsense, you are doing a great job. Look around you."

"But I didn't do any of this. Other people did."

"She's a gypsy," said Josh as his attention was glued on the lady.

The young girl had long black hair that bounced back and forth revealing a large earring in one ear. She had a brightly colored striped skirt with a hemline halfway between her knees and ankles. Over her white blouse was a vest made from material displaying bright flowers. In the girl's hair there was a red bandana and a white flower. Her wrists were burdened with numerous metal bracelets that jingled every time she moved her arms.

Dollie and Josh watched the girl as she made her way across the room. The girl stopped and appeared to ask for directions from some of the people. Margaret made her way to the girl and soon began pointing to the door leading to the kitchen. The gypsy made a quick exit thru the kitchen door. Dollie and Josh both rushed to Margaret's side.

"Maggie," they both began in unison. "What did she want and who is she?"

"She wanted to see the twins. What's up with that?" questioned Margaret.

"What would the twins have to do with her?" asked Josh.

"Maybe she is a cousin passing thru town?" suggested Dollie.

"Cousin of the twins—a fortuneteller—gypsy? I don't think so," muttered Margaret as she walked back to her position at the table.

"Don't look now but we are having quite a draw. There is Father Mickovech from St. Louis. Why would he be here? Just how much did you advertise this event?" asked Josh.

"Who did you say? Where?" said Dollie.

"Hey, did you see who is here," asked Margaret as she hastened back to talk to them. "Isn't that the priest who has a weekly program on television? Josh?"

"Why are you asking me? I do recognize him but have no idea about what he does?"

Father Mickovech was dressed in black except for a thin collar around the top of his shirt. He had a large chain with a big cross dangling around his neck. He wore a cape that made him look almost like Dracula and seemed to be floating as he walked.

"Yes, I do remember," blurted out Josh. "It was exorcism. I did a news article on him when I worked for the Chicago Tribune. That was ages ago."

"Exorcism?!!" shouted the two women in unison as they quickly tried to put their hand over the other woman's mouth to keep quiet. The women looked at each other and then at Josh.

"How remarkable that a man who is involved in exorcism has arrived at the church where rumors are circulating that it is haunted. This man enters right after a fortuneteller/gypsy woman has made an appearance. Here we are, ladies and gentlemen, in a church where rumors of ghosts are flying. Now there is a story!" Josh said.

Margaret in her excitement lost her balance. She tried to catch herself by grabbing hold of a box of merchandise on the nearby table. With a thud she landed on the old wooden floor and the box of items on top of her.

"Maggie! Are you alright?" Dollie said as she quickly went to Margaret's aid. "Maggie, are you ok?"

"Quite—hey, here is a ouiji board. I haven't seen one of these since college," answered a quickly recovering Margaret to cover her embarrassment in falling. Still laying on the floor she examined the box to see if the ouiji board was still intact.

"Never used one," commented Dollie as she helped Margaret up and put the box back on the table. "Are you sure you are alright?"

"Yes, we had a lot of fun with a ouiji board in college. It was during summer school. My sorority sisters had a weiner roast on the lake and one girl had brought the board. We gathered around the fire and were asking questions about our boyfriends. Next thing we knew we were using the board to get the answers."

"Did you get any good answers?" asked Josh with a laugh.

"Well, I married the guy I asked questions about and we all know that was a mistake," chuckled Margaret who was wrapped in too many memories to share.

Dollie stooped down and picked up another item. It was a glass pyramid with a string on it. She looked it over and allowed the pyramid to swing back and forth as she looked at it.

"Oh my, I want that!" said Margaret.

Dollie handed it to her and didn't get a chance to say another word before Margaret was headed for the cashier while clutching the box.

"That was strange," said Josh. "What do you think she plans to do with it?"

They both shrugged their shoulders as they watched Margaret pay and then speed over to the other side of the room. Dollie pulled Josh away from the tables and turned him toward the wall so she could talk privately with him.

She began to whisper, but was bumped into by someone on the floor.

"There should be a small triangular piece. Do you see it on the floor?"

Startled the two turned back around to see Margaret on the floor.

"Ah, what?" said Dollie in a startled voice. "Oh, I thought you were gone. A what?"

"Here it is!" rejoiced Margaret. "It is all here. You know, one girl asked that day at the lake if there was a devil. The board answered very quickly that he was round the corner of a boat house there at the lake. None of us got brave enough to go check."

Margaret had the ouiji board and box in hand and was headed for the door quickly disappearing from sight.

Josh and Dollie exchanged looks and smiled. They knew Margaret was unpredictable and she had proven it again. What would she be up to next?

CHAPTER TWELVE

A s the afternoon passed and the garage sale started winding down, it had been a well attended sale and most of what had been donated had been sold. Dollie slowly walked around the room surveying the remaining items. She would have to make plans for where the left over items would be stored until the next sale. She knew the congregation would expect the merchandise to be out of sight when church services started the next morning.

As Dollie walked around the multi-purpose room she noted that "her" table was gone. Her plan to buy the table back had been forgotten when Father Mickovech arrived. She wondered where he had gone so quickly. Even Josh didn't have a chance to talk to him.

The chair she bought for Rev. Temple was missing. She hoped Josh had taken it to her house. She could already imagine Jack stretched out in the recliner watching television. She thought to herself about sitting in a comfortable chair after spending much of the day on her feet.

"Maybe Jack will be gone counseling someone and I can get a chance to use the chair first," she thought.

Steve Elsea entered the room and spotting Dollie came her way. He had a man with him who was carrying a brief case and it was apparent that there was a problem.

"Hi, Steve," greeted Dollie.

"Dollie, we have a problem," began Steve.

Another problem was the last thing Dollie wanted to deal with now. The man was from the choir robe company and according to Steve's new information it took three or four months at the least to prepare the robes. Even if they ordered the robes tonight they wouldn't be able to get them before June. That would be well passed the Choir Festival event.

Lord, thank you for the donations and the customers. You have provided so much, but can you help us? Will you provide us a way to get our robes by next week. The people have worked so hard for us. We don't want to disappoint them. We trust you and praise your name. Amen.

Dollie walked into the sanctuary and decided to go to the choir loft to meditate as she had done a couple of years earlier. She felt the quietness would help her to clear her mind. Maybe there was something she was missing. Maybe there was a way to get robes from another church or school — used robes that were already made. They had the money and the desire to work something out. She would have to think.

With every step she took the stairs squeaked louder. Halfway up the stairs she began to hear groaning. A cold breeze began to blow across her face. It was not like the warm breeze she had felt when in the cemetery the day before when she felt the closeness of her husband, Howard. This breeze sent a chill down her back. She stopped to listen for the groan.

"Oh-h-h-h," it continued.

"Dollie's eyes got wider as she wondered what it could be or who. With a deep breath she began the climb of the stairs to the loft again. Each squeak brought her closer and each step her heart raced a little faster.

"Dollie," shouted Margaret. "Thank God it is you!"

"What are you doing up here?" asked Dollie.

"Well, er—ah," Margaret stammered. "I have Gwen, Jason and Suzy with me. We are talking to the ouiji board about the sounds we have been hearing lately."

Dollie's mouth dropped open. She couldn't believe that her best friend had gathered a group to talk to a ouiji board about spirits. Even more astonishing was that they were doing it in the choir loft of the church building.

"Have you lost your mind?" began Dollie. "Didn't you say to me, 'If Christ be for us who can be against us?'"

"Well, ah, I know," Margaret tried to answer. "I just thought when I saw that ouiji board that it couldn't hurt. We needed some answers."

Dollie walked over to the rest. She eyed each one of them as they looked at the board with deep concentration.

"You want to join us?" asked Suzy Kearns.

"I don't think she does," interrupted Margaret. "Maybe we should get out of here before God strikes us dead. Dollie is right. This is not the place and we are foolish to think that we should talk to the devil to get answers to what has been happening in the church building lately."

The group gathered their things and began making their way down the stairs. As they squeaked their way halfway down the stairs they suddenly started hearing shouts. Their eyes widened and their bodies started trembling. Dollie leaned over the railing of the loft to see what was going on. There was Father Mickovech waving his arms wildly and shouting. He walked across the platform where the pulpit was located shouting louder and waving his arms even wilder. With a grunt he leaped forward toward the pulpit and yelled again.

Margaret and her cohorts edged into the sanctuary and gazed in wonder at the sight of the man now prostrate across the pulpit. Dollie leaned over the balcony from the loft to see if there was someone with Father Mickovech. Standing at the edge of the curtains was Joan Stacy.

"Joan!" exclaimed a shocked Dollie. "Did you bring him here?"

"Something had to be done. We couldn't have a decent practice without some strange things happening. Let's face facts. This place is haunted or demons have taken over the church."

Margaret and her friends walked down to join Joan. Dollie straightened back up and then sat down on the front pew of the loft. She shook her head in disbelief that her friends were acting like pagans. She thought about the past few days. A simple little sound that she had heard earlier; a practical joke by Margaret; and an unusual power failure in the church building and what happens? The choir members desert their faith in Jesus Christ to follow every alternative. The whole group had allowed their minds to run wild.

"Something had to be done alright," Dollie thought to herself, "and it isn't calling in an astrologer or magician or any of these other people they had invited. Things needed to be discussed and focused and aimed back the right direction."

Dollie gathered strength and went down the stairs to join the choir members. As she reached them and was about to speak, the group heard a loud rattling in a side room. A humming voodoo like sound began. The group looked with fear at the door to the room as it began opening. The rattling sound and humming became louder.

"Hey, Ralph and Robert!" yelled Dollie, "Get out here!"

The door opened slowly and the twins peaked out as they said in unison, "Dollie? Is that you?"

"I saw the gypsy earlier in the day. She asked for you two and hearing the sounds I assumed it must be you two and the gypsy. Now get out here and sit down with the rest of them."

Ralph and Robert led the gypsy out of the side room and with a questioning look on their faces the whole group looked at each other and then started looking at the floor feeling guilty. Dollie looked the group over slowly. Shaking her head she turned her attention to the picture of Christ on the wall next to the hymn board.

"When did we lose sight of what we are doing?" she began. "We had achieved our dream of hosting the choir festival. We had brought glory to God through our singing and witnessing. We were swamped with the love and appreciation of a congregation and community as we sought to buy choir robes. We were determined to serve God. What happened? Here we are, a group turning to a ouiji board, exorcists, and gypsies. Makes you proud to be a part of Sassafras Springs and the Nickerson Street Church, doesn't it?"

The choir members were looking at the floor in disbelief that they could have been swept away from Jesus Christ. They admitted that they had been too proud of themselves when word was received about hosting the choir festival. God had chosen to bless them and they had chosen to think too highly of themselves and reject Him.

After a brief discussion, the group decided to call the choir members to the church for a meeting at 7 p.m. A frustrated Dollie explained the situation and what had happened over the past few days to the members of the board and to Rev. Temple. They were invited to participate in the meeting.

CHAPTER THIRTEEN

The members of the choir, the church board and a few extras met at 7 p.m. for their special meeting. Most arrived early and were eager to discuss what they thought had happened, but Dollie encouraged them to remain quiet until the meeting had begun. She promised to give each person an opportunity to speak.

Concerned about the strangers present, Dollie suggested to Rev. Temple that she thought it might be better to have a closed meeting. Jack assured her that the strangers had been invited by the board and were needed for the meeting. Dollie continued to question Rev. Temple's judgment and expressed that she thought it would be easier for the group to share their experiences with only the choir and board present. Again, Rev. Temple insisted that the strangers be present. Trusting him, Dollie called the meeting to order and instructed everyone to take a seat in the front of the sanctuary.

"Rev. Temple, would you open our meeting with prayer?" requested Dollie.

"Certainly," replied Rev. Temple as he lifted his hands signaling the group to stand for the prayer. "We lift our voices to you, oh Lord, and ask that you bless this meeting. We need answers to some puzzling questions. Help us to open our eyes and ears to find solutions. Help us to be patient with each other and united in spirit. For you, we do these things. Amen."

"Thank you, Rev. Temple," said Dollie as she turned her attention to the matter at hand. "I am directing this meeting tonight since I was selected to be director of the Choir Festival. We have only three weeks left to prepare and since we have had a few unusual matters develop, well, ah—this meeting has been called to deal with what needs to be dealt with. I am confident that together we can discover what has been going on."

Dollie took a deep breath and prepared to retell the entire story of the events of the past week. As she started to talk it occurred to her that maybe listing the events on a blackboard would be easier. The group could then examine what they thought had caused the different happenings. There had to be other explanations for what they thought had happened. She asked Rev. Temple to bring his chalk board into the sanctuary so they could use it.

"Choir," she began, "what was the first thing that happened the other night?"

"The lights went out," said Lincoln Madison.

"No, the door to the sanctuary came open and slammed against the wall," corrected Steve Elsea.

"We heard a crash of thunder and then the door slammed against the wall," said Emily Houseman.

"No, I think it was that sound that Dollie keeps hearing. I heard it too," said Margaret. "It went—oh, I don't know. It was some strange little sound like a chain moving."

"Alright," said Dollie as she wrote on the board.

Chain sound
Crash of thunder
Lights went out
Door slammed against wall

"Now what else happened?" Dollie asked.

"That light from the ceiling that was shining on the pulpit," added Ralph and Robert. "That was awesome—even if it nearly scared us to death!"

"T-t-there was the l-l-light on the st-st-stained glass window," stuttered Joan Stacy.

Chain sound
Crash of thunder
Lights went out
Door slammed against wall
Light from ceiling to pulpit
Light on stained glass window

"You forgot the cold breeze blowing over the entire building!" added Sherrie Bennett. "Remember how the curtains behind the pulpit lifted up?"

"That's right," shuttered Ralph and Robert. "That really scared us. I thought spirits were taking over."

"Yes," began Dollie. "That's why we are here. We know what we saw and what we thought happened. We need to analyze the situations and find out what really happened? Before we leave tonight we will all laugh at our foolishness and be assured that this mystery is solved."

"Remember the tapping and the occasional whining?" asked Steve Elsea. "And the cold—it was really getting cold in the building by the time we left. Put that on the list."

Chain sound
Crash of thunder
Lights went out
Door slammed against wall
Light from ceiling to pulpit
Light on stained glass window
Cold breeze blowing across the room
Curtains behind pulpit lifted up
Tapping and whining sounds
Temperature dropped and made room cold

"Well, is there anything else?" asked Dollie. After a moment of silence she turned to the blackboard and began writing. She added "We have quite a list, but I have a few more things to add."

The choir became consumed by pride
The choir allowed fear to replace reason
The choir failed to keep their faith in Christ as their foundation

Each member of the choir sat quietly with their heads down. They remembered how excited they had been a week earlier. They had been boastful about their abilities the night Rev. Temple announced they were going to host the festival. In an instant they lost sight of the mission of the choir. Instead they were filled with pride and now found themselves humbled because of their lack of faith in Christ.

Dollie shared with them how all of them had been good examples for her in different ways and at different times. She was confused now that the choir members had turned to ouiji boards, gypsies and exorcists instead of praying to God for answers.

"What happened to us?" she asked.

The choir remained quiet. After a few moments Dollie began by saying, "Now think. Don't just start talking. Who has a realistic answer for what caused one of these items on our list?"

"Bill, why are you here?" asked Steve as he looked around the room and saw Bill Owens of Owens' Electrical. "Did you have something to do with the blackout?"

"Yes, I was underneath the building putting in some new wiring for the additional air conditioning units being installed," he answered.

"Air conditioning?" said the choir members in unison. "If you turned the new units on while we were here that would explain why it got very cold in the building."

"It also explains why the curtain started blowing behind the pulpit," said Rev. Temple. "There's a new vent by the chair where I sit on Sundays. I was examining the new vents and where they were blowing. It scared me at first as the breeze was approaching hurricane proportions."

The choir members and board all laughed at the exaggeration as Rev. Temple continued. "Bill returned the air conditioning unit Mr. Walters had ordered for us and got a smaller one. We could have frozen to death with that thing going full blast."

The choir laughed again. Dollie took some chalk and marked out the lines that said:

Temperature dropped and made room cold
Curtains behind pulpit lifted up
Cold breeze blowing across the room

"Are there any others that the air conditioning explains?" asked Dollie.

"I suspect the door flew open and slammed against the wall because of the breeze made by the air conditioning," suggested Sherrie Bennett.

"Exactly!" the choir members shouted in unison.

"Now we are making progress," encouraged Dollie. "What is next?"

"What could have caused the 'crash of thunder?'" asked Steve. "We now know that there were no clouds, no storm, and no rain outside. The sound had to be something inside."

"Almost," interrupted John Macon. "I was here installing your air conditioning unit. When we were unloading the replacement unit we knocked some metal siding off the truck. It made quite a loud rumble as it hit the concrete walk in back. I had a headache for a few minutes."

The group laughed again and pointed at the board with motions to mark **Crash of thunder** with a line.

"We know that the lights went out several times and that was because of Bill's rewiring," began Margaret. "That doesn't explain what the light from the ceiling to the pulpit was. You didn't install a new spotlight up there, did you? I can't see anything. So, ah, where did it come from?"

"I didn't do any wiring in the ceiling," responded Bill Owens.

"Nor did we," added the air conditioning men.

"Wait a minute," began Rev. Temple. "What if the light went from the pulpit to the ceiling rather than from the ceiling to the pulpit?"

There was a moment of silence as the group thought about the possibility. Steve walked to the platform and began examining the pulpit area closely. After a few minutes Lincoln joined him. They looked at the ceiling and then again at the pulpit.

"What is this?" asked Steve.

"That's the microphone for the speaker system," answered Dollie as she looked over his shoulder. "Wait a minute. I don't remember it looking like that."

"It does now," broke in Rev. Temple. "We had a new system installed."

"That's great and in time for the festival. Did you say both a new air conditioning unit and a new sound system— both? How did we afford it?" asked Lincoln.

"Mr. Walters at the bank made the donation when he got the refund after we returned the too large air conditioning unit. Said we could use the money for anything else we needed. So naturally we replaced the speaker system," reported Rev. Temple.

"You must have really touched his heart recently. He doesn't do that kind of thing very often," commented Bill Owens.

"So, where did the light come from?" repeated Margaret.

The group continued to examine the pulpit and the ceiling. Finally after no one was able to supply a logical answer Dollie said to skip that statement for a while. The group then turned their attention to the stained glass window incident.

"It was breathtakingly beautiful," agreed the choir members as they remembered that night. "It scared us all, but we were still in awe of its beauty."

"I nearly passed out," began Joan Stacy.

"Yes, I remember that," said Margaret. "I thought you were going to have a heart attack. It scared all of us. You were pale as a ghost."

They laughed at the choice of "ghost" to describe Joan. Dollie rolled her eyes as she groaned and turned her attention to Joan.

"So, Joan," questioned Dollie, "What was your problem?"

"I know most of you don't remember Sidney Smith," explained Joan. "He was my husband."

"What?" said the choir members in unison as none of them knew she had been married.

"I took my maiden name back when we were divorced. He got mixed up in some scandal in New York and well— things got messy. Yes, I know you thought I was an unwed mother, but it was to protect the child. Things were compli- cated and dangerous then."

"How did he come to give the window to the church?" asked Lincoln Madison.

"The day he gave the window to the church would have been our first wedding anniversary. He knew he was going to prison and he wanted to get right with God—and with me. He didn't know if he could survive prison life and figured he wouldn't live to be with me again so he insisted on our getting a divorce. He wanted me to be free to come home and live an ordinary life. He wanted me free of his 'disgraceful behavior,' as he put it. It nearly killed me. We were so much in love and not even married three months. I hadn't told my family about the marriage so no one was going to know that I was married to him if I didn't tell them."

"That must have been painful for you?" remarked Colleen.

"He picked the picture of 'Jesus as the good shepherd' to let me know he was asking Jesus to watch over me."

The choir smiled at her approvingly as they thought about a man so romantic as to buy an expensive stained glass window with such a caring message.

"I told no one. My brother suspected something one time when I got a letter from a New York law firm concerning Sidney. Maybe he knew and just didn't say anything. I don't know. We have not been close since I came back from New York."

"I bet one of the workers the other night took the oppor- tunity to clean the outside of the window when we were installing that outside light. The ladders were available. It probably had never been washed before. That would explain why it was so beautiful," suggested Mary Lynn Sumner.

"That doesn't explain the light on the window," reminded Dollie. "There has never been a light shining on the window. Even the sun doesn't hit it because of its location. Any ideas?"

"Don't you people know what is going on here?" asked Bill Owens, the electrician. "I installed two new lights in the parking lot. They are controlled by movement. When someone is walking to their car the lights come on. After they are gone the lights go off. Someone must have been moving around in the parking lot when you were in the choir loft and the light came on. Guess that would have scared me if I was standing in complete darkness and then suddenly was immersed by a light I didn't know existed."

The group laughed again and motioned for Dollie to draw a line across the **Light on stained glass window.**

"By the way," began Bill again. "After thinking about it I may have a solution to the light from the ceiling to the pulpit and the whining noise. I was tapping around underneath the floor to locate the proper location for the wires for the new sound system. The whine could have been my drill when I was drilling a hole to put the wires thru. I had turned the lights off in the sanctuary, but had pulled an extension cord underneath the floor with me. I had a light on it. Could it be that the light from the extension was shining thru the new hole I had drilled in the floor?"

Steve jumped up and examined where the wires came out of the floor. With his hand he focused where the light had been seen and where it would come from if it had come from underneath the floor. The paths fit. The choir now knew what had caused the light from the ceiling to the pulpit. Dollie drew a line thru two more of the items listed. The only one left on the list was the chain sound that she had heard that started the whole mysterious week.

"One item left," said Dollie. "Anyone else have an idea?"

The group remained silent.

"Hm-m-m?" the group said together. "Let's pray."

The group prayed and left the meeting stronger than when they had come. They were determined to remain dedicated to Christ. Despite not locating the strange sound they knew the festival would be a spirited event because they were letting the Holy Spirit lead.

As Dollie shut the outside door of the church building she heard the lock click.

"And no strange sound when it closes?" she chuckled. "Thank you, Lord."

She went over the events of the week as she walked to her car with a bounce in her step again. "So simple were the answers to such craziness. What fools we were...., but everything seems right with the world now. Thank you, Lord."

For a moment she stood looking at the beautiful yard the congregation had raked, mowed, and landscaped during the week. She sighed with relief again that the mysteries had been solved. As she started her old blue Plymouth she remembered here strange noise and again felt good that she had not heard it all afternoon.

"Maybe it's gone," she thought.

CHAPTER FOURTEEN

Dollie pulled the car into the driveway at her house at 10:30 p.m. and was quick to make her way to the back door. She was eager to tell Uncle John the results of the meeting. What a laugh she expected he would have listening to all the silliness. She was glad he was there and that they could share some ice cream while talking about the week's events.

She noticed the light was on in the guest room and was surprised to find Uncle John with dust mop in hand. Being the thoughtful man he was, Uncle John knew that Dollie's son and family were coming the next week for a visit and he was going to be sure that the room was ready. She looked around and nodded approvingly and then insisted he come out to the kitchen for some ice cream. He quickly put the mop down and was on his way.

She dropped her keys on the kitchen table and walked into the living room. There was Rev. Temple asleep in the new recliner. His chair had been delivered by Josh just like she had hoped. The new chair was setting beside "her" table that mysteriously disappeared at the garage sale. She was glad to see that it had shown up exactly where she had wanted it for the past several months. It fit perfectly in front of the picture window. In the center of the table was a bouquet of tulips in the vase her mother had given her several years earlier—just as she had imagined it.

"That Josh," she mumbled. "What am I going to do with him?"

She smiled a big smile as she covered Rev. Temple with the afghan she had bought at the sale made by Julia Ferguson. She would leave him to enjoy his chair. He had worked hard all day at the sale and needed rest for Sunday services the next day.

Thank you, Lord, for showing us the way. Your strength fills me and keeps me. Your love overflows. May you always be praised here in Sassafras Springs, Amen

"Cling-chink!" went the strange sound.

Dollie let out a shriek. Uncle John, coughing, sprang from his chair.

"What was that?" he yelled. "Dollie, are you alright?"

"The noise is here! I don't believe it! I must be cursed."

Uncle John put his arm around Dollie and tried to calm her down. She was trembling. She looked around the house and wondered how the noise could be in her house. What was it? How could it have followed her home?

"Hey, what is all the commotion?' asked Rev. Temple who had been awakened by Dollie's scream.

"Pull yourself together," said Uncle John.

"Did you hear it, Jack," asked Dollie.

"Hear what? All I heard was your scream. What is wrong?" responded Rev. Temple.

"Tha-tha-that noise—. The noise I have been hearing in the chur-chur-church building is he-he-here.," Dollie stammered as she continued to shake with fear. "Am I going crazy?"

She looked frantically at Uncle John who was as wide-eyed as he could get wondering what was wrong with Dollie. He reached for the broom in the corner and raised it like he would use it as a weapon.

"Just lead me to it," he said. "I'll protect you."

"It sounded like it was coming from the kitchen," Dollie said as she was beginning to regain her composure.

Together Uncle John and Dollie peeked around the corner of the door to see into the kitchen while Rev. Temple took a tour of the room to reassure them it was safe. The two crept slowly into the kitchen while Rev. Temple got a couple of dishes and spoons and placed them on the table.

"Did someone say something about ice cream?" asked Rev. Temple.

"I'll get it," said Dollie as she began to assert some confidence again.

"Alright," began Uncle John as he waved the broom in the air. "Where are you? Give up! We're on to you!"

"What are you doing, Uncle John?" laughed Dollie.

Uncle John looked at her and laughed too. The three of them sat down at the table and scooped ice cream into their individual bowls. It was cookie dough ice cream tonight.

"We just prayed and celebrated strength in Jesus at the church and here I am a few minutes later scared to death in my own house of some crazy sound. Doesn't that take the cake?" she laughed.

"That's what we need," said Rev. Temple.

"What?" said a startled Dollie.

"Take what cake?" said Uncle John with a grumble. "We may be in danger and you're laughing."

"No, Uncle John—," laughed Dollie.

"No, I meant we needed a bit of cake with this ice cream. And just by chance I bought one today at the sale. I'll be right back," said Rev. Temple as he got up and disappeared to his part of the house.

"Uncle John, let me assure you we are not in danger," responded Dollie. "We just went over the entire church building finding explanations for all of the strange noises and experiences we had in the past week. Everything was explained except this strange sound that now has moved to this house. There was no ghost at church and there is no ghost here. Just a peculiar sound that we have not identified, but we will. Now let's be logical. What was at church that now has been moved here besides me? Do you know of anything?"

"Well," said Uncle John said as he turned his attention away from being scared to being the conqueror. "I didn't notice that you brought anything home with you except the notebook you laid on the television. You don't think you could have something in it?"

They went to the television and opened the notebook. Dollie took everything out of it. She examined her pen and then shook the entire notebook to see if anything would fall out of it. Just when she was satisfied that everything was alright with it—."

"Cling-chink!"

Uncle John's eyes popped open and he gasped. He glanced around the living room and raised the broom and took a swipe through the air. Dollie burst out laughing when Uncle John's broom came around a second time and struck Rev. Temple in the shoulder.

"Hey, watch it!" said Rev. Temple as he tried to duck the second swing of the broom while balancing the cake with one hand.

"It sounds like it is coming from the kitchen. It must be in there. Let's sit down in the kitchen and have some cake and maybe a little dip of ice cream on top," suggested Dollie.

"What? Did something happen while I was gone? When I left you seconds ago you were enjoying yourselves in the kitchen and here you are uptight and in the living room.

I'm guessing you heard the sound again," questioned Rev. Temple.

"It's real," added Uncle John. "I heard it this time."

The three of them went back into the kitchen and cut Rev. Temple's cake. It was pumpkin cake with a creamed cheese frosting. They added a dip of butter pecan ice cream.

"Hmmmm, this is good," remarked Rev. Temple as he took a finger, wiped up some icing and put it in his mouth.

"You are as bad as a little kid," laughed Dollie.

The three of them started laughing and telling stories as they enjoyed the cake, ice cream and conversation. No sound came and they were ending their day with a good fun moment together. Dollie and Jack went over the events of the meeting again to help Uncle John understand everything. Finally convinced that they had driven the sounds out of the house with their confident rational logical thinking processes they stood and looked at each other with a nod of approval that everything was alright.

"Cling-chink!"

The three of them looked at each other again and without a word they headed to their separate bedrooms. No one said aloud that they had heard the sound. Dollie decided that the next morning would bring answers that the late hour would only leave confused. Uncle John thought he would double check the doors to make sure they were all locked. Rev. Temple decided he would review his sermons for the next day.

As Uncle John checked the front door one more time he remembered that Colleen had come by earlier and left two teddy bears for Dollie. He tapped on Dollie's bedroom door.

In a shaky voice Dollie said, "Who is it?"

"Just me," said Uncle John. "I forgot to tell you. Colleen brought by some teddy bears she said you planned to use in the centerpiece for the refreshment table at the choir festival."

"Great, I had forgotten about them," laughed Dollie. "I will have to thank Colleen tomorrow. They are the cutest things. Remind me to show you in the morning. Thanks and have a good night."

"Good night."

The lights went out all over the house as they went to bed preparing for another busy day on Sunday. Prayers had been said. The sound of snoring could be heard rather quickly from Uncle John's room.

"What a minute?" said Dollie out loud as she sat up in bed.

Her door opened and she quickly began stumbling around in the dark as she made her way to the kitchen. Rev. Temple turned a light on in the hall to see what was going on.

"Everything alright?" he asked.

"Hey, who is that?" hollered Uncle John. "I've got a weapon. You get out of here!"

"Uncle John, you better not have a weapon in my house. This is Dollie. Wake up and get in here. You too, Jack."

The three of them met in the kitchen again. Dollie asked Uncle John where he had put the teddy bears and requested he get them for her. Rev. Temple looked puzzled but was confident that Dollie had something important to show them. Uncle John returned with the teddy bears and placed them in the center of the kitchen table.

Dollie took one of them and examined it. She turned it on and demonstrated how it worked. Both men agreed the bears were cute, but asked why she decided to show them dancing bears at this hour of the night when they could see them just as well in the morning.

"These bears were at the church every time that the sound was heard. Now they are here in this house where we are hearing that same noise. This has to be the connection. The sound is coming from them."

The two men looked at each other convinced that Dollie had lost it. She insisted they sit down and wait a few minutes to see if she was right.

"Well, I'm not eating any more cake or ice cream. I'm stuffed," laughed Rev. Temple. "So you think this is what makes that sound. That is rather interesting."

"Ok, you two go to bed. I'll stay and listen," she said realizing they did need to be in bed. "I just want this noise thing settled."

"No, I'll stay. I'll be glad to get this noise thing settled too," laughed Rev. Temple.

So they sat down and waited. They occasionally paced the floor. Uncle John shuffled thru the newspaper again. Then twenty minutes later there was a sound made by the bears.

"Cling-chink!"

"Aha!" they all shouted in unison as they stood, rejoiced and headed for bed.

The next day Colleen called to tell Dollie that the Weinberg's had asked if the bears had sold for a good price. The woman also shared that the bears made a funny noise every so often if a switch on the battery is not turned off. The sound had tricked her into having their water heater inspected and was quite an embarrassment when the repairman discovered that the noise had come from the bears.

Dollie laughed and rejoiced at God's eternal goodness saying, "If God is for us, who can be against us."

Printed in the United States
220008BV00001B/6/P

9 781607 916758